Pelican Books
Constantine and the Conversion of Europe

A. H. M. Jones was Professor of Ancient History at Cambridge University and a Fellow of Jesus College, Cambridge, from 1951 until his death in 1970. He was born in 1904 and educated at Cheltenham College and New College, Oxford. From 1926 to 1946 he was a Fellow of All Souls, Oxford. In 1927 he began a series of excavations at Constantinople and Jerash, and until 1934 he was Reader in Ancient History at the Egyptian University in Cairo. Returning to Oxford he became Lecturer in Ancient History at Wadham College, and from 1949 to 1951 he was Professor of Ancient History at University College, London.

His other books are: *The Cities of the Eastern Roman Provinces* (1937), *The Herods of Judaea* (1938), *The Greek City from Alexander to Justinian* (1940), *Athenian Democracy* (1957), *Studies in Roman Government and Law* (1960), *The Later Roman Empire* (1964), in four volumes, *The Decline of the Ancient World* (1966), *Sparta* (1966), *A History of Rome Through the Fifth Century* (1968), *Augustus* (1970), and, with J. R. Martindale and John Morris, *The Prosopography of the Later Roman Empire Vol I* (1971).

Constantine and the
Conversion of Europe

A. H. M. Jones

Penguin Books

Penguin Books Ltd, Harmondsworth,
Middlesex, England
Penguin Books Australia Ltd, Ringwood,
Victoria, Australia

First published in the 'Teach Yourself History'
series by The English Universities Press 1949
Revised edition published in the U.S.A. by
Collier Books 1962
Published in Pelican Books 1972

Made and printed in Great Britain by
C. Nicholls & Company Ltd
Set in Linotype Pilgrim

A General Introduction to the 'Teach Yourself History' Series

This series has been undertaken in the conviction that there can be no subject of study more important than history. Great as have been the conquests of natural science in our time – such that many think of ours as a scientific age *par excellence* – it is even more urgent and necessary that advances should be made in the social sciences, if we are to gain control of the forces of nature loosed upon us. The bed out of which all the social sciences spring is history; there they find, in greater or lesser degree, subject-matter and material, verification or contradiction.

There is no end to what we can learn from history, if only we will, for it is coterminous with life. Its special field is the life of man in society, and at every point we can learn vicariously from the experience of others before us in history.

To take one point only – the understanding of politics: how can we hope to understand the world of affairs around us if we do not know how it came to be what it is? How to understand Germany, or Soviet Russia, or the United States – or ourselves, without knowing something of their history?

There is no subject that is more useful, or indeed indispensable.

Some evidence of the growing awareness of this may be seen in the immense increase in the interest of the reading public in history and the much larger place the subject has come to take in education in our time.

This series has been planned to meet the needs and demands of a very wide public and of education – they are indeed the same. I am convinced that the most congenial, as well as the most concrete and practical, approach to history is the biographical, through the lives of the great men whose actions have been so much part of history, and whose careers in turn have been so moulded and formed by events.

The key-idea of this series, and what distinguishes it from any other that has appeared, is the intention by way of a biography of a great man to open up a significant historical theme; for example, Cromwell and the Puritan Revolution, or Lenin and the Russian Revolution.

My hope is, in the end, as the series fills out and completes itself, by a sufficient number of biographies to cover whole periods and subjects in that way. To give you the history of the United States, for example, or the British Empire or France, *via* a number of biographies of their leading historical figures.

That should be something new, as well as convenient and practical, in education.

I need hardly say that I am a strong believer in people with good academic standards writing once more for the general reading public, and of the public being given the best that the universities can provide. From this point of view this series is intended to bring the university into the homes of the people.

A. L. Rowse
All Souls College, Oxford

Contents

Introduction

The early historians of the Church had a habit which is very useful to posterity. Owing presumably to their reverence for the actual words of holy writ, they developed the habit of citing their authorities in full even when they were not inspired. Hence we possess a relatively large number of documents from the age of Constantine – imperial constitutions and edicts, synodical letters of church councils, and letters written by bishops and, most interesting of all, by Constantine himself.

Some of these documents are preserved in the works of contemporary authors: Lactantius, whose little pamphlet, *On the Deaths of the Persecutors*, is, despite its violent prejudice, an invaluable firsthand record of events from the accession of Diocletian to the death of Maximin; Athanasius, who many years after the event wrote up the story of the ecclesiastical struggles of his youth in a series of polemical tracts, the most important of which is *The Defence against the Arians*; and, above all, Eusebius. To Eusebius we owe two historical works, his great *Church History*, the last three books of which give an eye-witness account of the Great Persecution, with a particularly valuable appendix giving full details for his own province of Palestine, and what is usually called his *Life of Constantine*, though it professes to be, and is, a long obituary or appreciation, bringing out its hero's achievements for Christianity.

Other documents are cited by later writers. Augustine, who was a keen controversialist against the Donatists, quotes a number in his letters and tracts against the sect, and a contemporary African bishop, Opatus, adds a whole appendix of documents to his book on the Donatist dispute. The fifth-century ecclesiastical historians, Socrates, Sozomen, Theodoret and Gelasius, cite between them a large number of documents dealing mainly with the Arian controversy. There are also a number of detached documents in collections of canons of ecclesiastical councils: some of these, known only from Syriac translations, have only come to light relatively recently.

Compared with the ecclesiastical sources, the secular are meagre. Of contemporary documents, the most important are a number of complimentary speeches addressed to the Emperor – naturally to be read with more than one grain of salt – and the great collection of imperial enactments, beginning with Constantine's capture of Rome, contained in the Theodosian Code. There are a few inscriptions, and the vast series of imperial coins, whose types and legends represent the propaganda of the emperors. There is only one secular historian even remotely worthy of the name whose works have survived – the fifth-century pagan Zosimus, who is violently prejudiced against the first Christian emperor. The rest are bald summaries and chronicles.

From the documents it is often possible to reconstruct the true sequence of events, when the narrative in which they are incorporated has gone wrong, either from the prejudice of the author or his sources, or from mere forgetfulness; for one can see that Augustine, for instance, had no very clear idea of the historical development of the Donatist controversy, and often cannot precisely date a document which he has in his hands. And, what is more interesting for our purpose, we can trace the development

of Constantine's religious thought in letters which he himself wrote and edicts which he himself issued.

It is only fair to warn the reader that the authenticity of
most of these documents has at one time or another been
challenged. The tide of 'higher criticism' was until recently receding, but of late there has been a backwash, and
the whole of Eusebius' *Life of Constantine*, and not merely
the documents in it, has been alleged to be a forgery of an
unknown writer fifty years later than Eusebius. The question is technical and I cannot argue it here, but I remain
completely unconvinced. Since I wrote the above I have
been able to adduce incontrovertible evidence that the
documents in the *Life of Constantine* are genuine (see
Journal of Ecclesiastical History, V, 1954, pp. 196-200), and
the authenticity of the *Life* itself has been vindicated by a
number of scholars.

Another line of criticism is that Constantine's edicts
and letters were drafted for him, and therefore do not give
a true picture of his thought. This is *a priori* improbable;
for all the evidence goes to show that conscientious Roman
emperors in general themselves drafted all important letters and edicts, and that their secretariats handled only
routine and formal matters. And Constantine's documents
in particular seem, to my judgement, to have a very personal and characteristic touch. They all breathe an earnest-
ness of belief and a certain violence of temper, which is
incidentally found in a number of his secular laws. And
they are written in a uniformly turgid and long-winded
style – the style of a semi-educated man such as Constantine was – which shows up even through Eusebius' Greek
translations, being markedly different from that of the
surrounding narrative.

The reader should also be warned that the narrative, as
I have reconstructed it from the documents, is in many
parts somewhat hypothetical, and that there are legitimate

differences of opinion between scholars as to the precise order of events in, for instance, the Donatist controversy and the sequel of the Council of Nicaea. I have thought it best to give a straight narrative without too many qualifying 'probablys' and 'perhapses'.

My thanks are due to Professor Norman Baynes and Professor Hugh Last, both of whom read this work in typescript and made a number of valuable suggestions and corrections: they are not responsible for any views expressed, particularly as I ventured to differ from them on several important points. I also wish to thank Professor Andrade for giving me the scientific explanation of Constantine's vision.

Map of the Roman Empire

A.D. 306 to 337

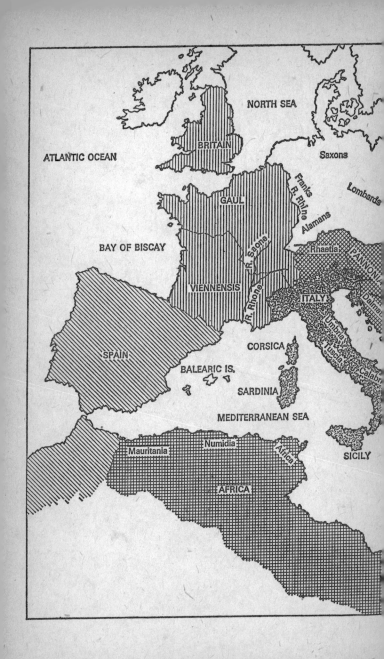

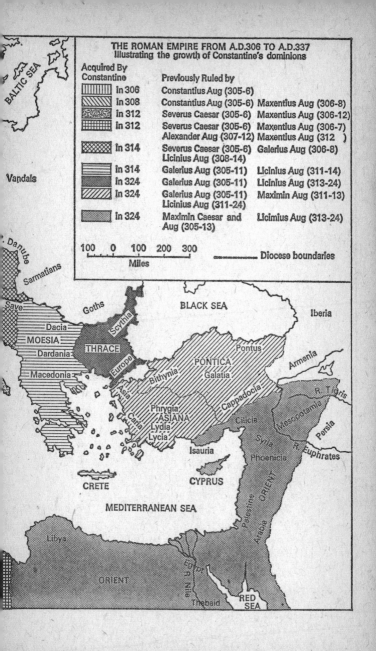

THE ROMAN EMPIRE FROM A.D.306 TO A.D.337
Illustrating the growth of Constantine's dominions

Acquired By Constantine
	Previously Ruled by
in 306	Constantius Aug (305-6)
in 308	Constantius Aug (305-6) Maxentius Aug (306-8)
in 312	Severus Caesar (305-6) Maxentius Aug (306-12)
in 312	Severus Caesar (305-6) Maxentius Aug (306-7) Alexander Aug (307-12) Maxentius Aug (312)
in 314	Severus Caesar (305-6) Galerius Aug (306-8) Licinius Aug (308-14)
in 314	Galerius Aug (305-11) Licinius Aug (311-14)
in 324	Galerius Aug (305-11) Licinius Aug (313-24)
in 324	Galerius Aug (305-11) Maximin Aug (311-13) Licinius Aug (311-24)
in 324	Maximin Caesar and Aug (305-13) Licinius Aug (313-24)

100   0   100   200   300   — — — — Diocese boundaries
Miles

BALTIC SEA

Vandals

R. Danube
Sarmatians
Save
Goths
Dacia
MOESIA
Dardania
Macedonia
Scythia
THRACE
Europe
Asia
Caria
Phrygia
ASIANA
Lydia
Lycia
Bithynia
PONTICA
Galatia
Pontus
Cappadocia
Isauria
Cilicia

BLACK SEA
Iberia
Armenia
R. Tigris
Mesopotamia
Persia
Syria
Phoenicia
R. Euphrates

CRETE
CYPRUS
ORIENT
Palestine
Arabia

MEDITERRANEAN SEA

Libya
ORIENT
Egypt
R. Nile
Thebaid
RED SEA

The Crisis of the Empire

Constantine was born at Naissus, the modern Nish, in Serbia. His father, Flavius Constantius, was an officer in the Roman army, and had already risen high in the service, perhaps to the rank of governor of a province. He was a native of Dardania (southern Serbia), and, according to later writers, of a noble Dardanian family. This is probably, however, mere courtly flattery; Constantius was no doubt, like all his later colleagues, of peasant birth, and had, like them, risen from the ranks – in the Roman army of that day every private carried the imperial purple in his knapsack. Constantine's mother, Helena, was, by universal consent, of the humblest origin, according to the commonest story, a barmaid.

The future emperor was born on 17 February: this we know, because his birthday was later a public holiday. But the year of birth is uncertain. According to his biographer, Eusebius, he had, when he died in 337, lived about twice as long as he had reigned – which was close to thirty-one years – and in another passage Eusebius declares that he lived twice as long as Alexander the Great, who died at the age of thirty-two. On this basis Constantine would have been born between 273 and 275. But there are a number of reliable indications, each slight in itself, but cumulatively convincing, that Constantine was considerably, perhaps as much as ten years, younger. Eusebius' exaggeration is tendentious – in both passages he is enumerating the blessings which God bestowed on the first Christian emperor – but it is excusable in an age in which there was no regular registration of births: it is likely enough that Constantine himself did not know precisely in what year he was born.

Whatever the exact date of his birth, Constantine was born in evil times. Many must have despaired of the future of the Empire, ravaged by civil wars and barbarian invasions, exhausted by ever-increasing requisitions, and depopulated by famines and plagues. The root cause of the troubles which had for two generations overwhelmed the empire lay in the indiscipline of the army and the political ambitions of its leaders. The famous year of the four emperors, A.D. 69, had taught the armies that an emperor could be made elsewhere than in Rome, but for over a century they did not exploit this knowledge. The second great civil war, which followed the murder of Commodus in 192, had more serious consequences. Septimius Severus, the winner in the conflict, knowing that his power depended on the goodwill of the armies, raised their pay, increased their privileges, and by freely promoting soldiers to administrative posts militarized the whole government. His last words to his sons are said to have been, 'Agree with each other, enrich the soldiers and never mind all the others,' and Caracalla, having murdered his brother, obeyed the other two precepts. But the troops had by now realized that they were the masters, and in 217 a military pronunciamento overthrew Caracalla. In the next thirty-six years there were twelve emperors (not counting co-regents), not one of whom died in his bed, and after the accession of Valerian in 253, it becomes impossible to keep count. In every quarter of the Empire the local armies proclaimed emperors: in Gaul there were five local emperors between 257 and 273, and between 260 and 273 Odenath, a citizen of Palmyra, and his widow Zenobia, ruled the eastern provinces from Asia Minor to Egypt. With the accession of Aurelian in 270 a recovery began, and the local pretenders were one by one suppressed. But he was assassinated in 275, his successor Tacitus lasted only six months, Probus, after a vigorous reign of six years, fell victim to another mutiny in 282, and Carus reigned only two years before he, too, was assassinated.

To add to the misfortunes of the Empire, the pressure of the Germans on the Rhine and Danube frontiers was increasing during this period. We now hear for the first time of two confederations of tribes, the Franks on the Lower Rhine and the Alamans on the Upper Rhine and Danube, who were to play a large part in the ultimate collapse of Roman authority in the West, and of the Goths, who occupied the Lower Danube, whence they invaded the Balkan provinces and the Crimea, which they made their base for piratical raids on Asia Minor. During this period, too, a new peril arose on the eastern frontier, when in 226 the feeble Arsacid dynasty of Parthia was overthrown by Artaxerxes, who claimed descent from the ancient Achaemenid kings of Persia, revived the national religion, Zoroastrianism, and laid claim to all the territories which Darius had ruled more than seven hundred years before. Distracted as they were by their perpetual civil wars, it is surprising that the emperors were as successful as they were in dealing with external enemies. But despite all their efforts, hordes of Germans constantly broke through the frontiers and ranged over Gaul, Illyricum, Thrace, and sometimes even Italy, looting and burning; while on several occasions Persian armies swept over Syria, and in 260 a Roman emperor, Valerian, was taken prisoner by the Persians.

To the horrors of war was added financial chaos. The maintenance of a standing army had always proved a strain on the primitive economy of the Roman Empire, and its budgets had been balanced with difficulty. Severus and Caracalla substantially increased the rates of pay and discharge gratuities, and the army was constantly growing as fresh units were raised by the emperors, either against their rivals or to meet the increasing pressure on the frontiers. Yet almost nothing was done to increase revenue: the only substantial increase in taxation was effected by Caracalla in 212, when, by granting Roman citizenship to all free inhabitants of the Empire, he made everyone liable to the inheritance tax which Augustus had imposed on Roman citizens. The assessment of the tribute, the direct tax on land and other property, was so complicated and rigid that it was left unaltered. Instead of raising further taxes the emperors preferred the easier path of depreciating the currency. The result was inflation. In an age when the currency was produced, not by the printing press, but by the hard labour of smiths, inflation could not achieve the speed of modern times, but over the years its cumulative effect was serious. Its extent can be gauged from the fact that the *denarius*, which had been in the latter part of the second century a decently engraved coin of more or less pure silver, had by the end of the third century become a roughly shaped lump of bronze, thinly washed in silver. In the early third century it was tariffed at 1,250 to the pound of gold; by 301 the official rate was 50,000.

The effect of the inflation on the population is difficult to estimate, but it was probably not catastrophic. The vast majority of the inhabitants of the Empire were peasants: those who owned their plots would have profited from the rise in the price of agricultural produce, and the greater number who were tenants would not have suffered, since their rents, being normally fixed by five-year leases, would tend to lag behind prices. The shopkeepers and manual workers who formed the proletariat of the towns need not have been seriously affected, for the former would naturally raise their prices, and the latter were mostly independent craftsmen who fixed their own terms with their customers. The upper and middle classes, the millionaires who formed the senatorial order, the equestrian order from which the great mass of the higher officials were drawn, and the many thousands of decurions who filled the town councils of the Empire, all had the bulk of their wealth invested in land. Some part they farmed themselves, or rather through bailiffs, employing slave labour supplemented by casual hired workers or the services of their tenants; the bulk was let to small tenants, either for a money rent or on the *métayage* system for a quota of the crop. Besides land, the only regular form of investment was mortgages. Mortgages would have been swallowed by the inflation, but income from directly farmed land and from rents in kind would have risen with the rise in prices, and money rents could be put up every five years. As a whole, therefore, the propertied classes would have suffered little, though no doubt some families, which had invested excessively in mortgages, or could not adjust their rents sufficiently rapidly to their rising scales of expenditure, were ruined, and the profiteers of the age, men who had made fortunes in government service, snapped up their estates.

The party most severely hit by the inflation was the government itself, and its salaried and wage-earning servants, more particularly the lower civil servants and the rank and file of the army, who had no other resource than their pay. Taxes brought in only the same nominal amount; the pay therefore of civil servants and soldiers could not be raised, and they found that it bought them less and less. Soldiers could, and did, help themselves by looting, and civil servants by corruption and extortion: it was during this period that the custom grew up whereby civil servants charged fees to the public for every act they performed – even the tax collector demanded a fee from the taxpayer for the favour of granting a receipt. On its side the government, though it did not raise the regular scale of pay, distributed special bonuses, or donatives, at more and more frequent intervals. Such donatives had long been customary on the accession of an emperor, and on special occasions such as triumphs. Now that emperors succeeded one another so rapidly, donatives naturally became more frequent. Should any emperor survive five years, it became customary to celebrate the event with a donative. The money for these distributions was procured by the 'free-will offerings' of the senate, and the 'crown money' voted by all the town councils of the Empire; these, being arbitrary exactions, could be increased in nominal value as the currency fell, or collected in gold bullion. And in the second place the government made free issues of rations and of uniforms both to the troops and to the civil service, obtaining the necessary supplies by requisitioning them from the public. By the end of the third century, rations (*annona*) had become, apart from irregular donatives, the substantial part of a soldier's or civil servant's pay, so much so that officers and higher officials were granted double or multiple rations, the surplus from which, after maintaining their families and slaves, they could sell back to the public. Requisitions in kind (also called *annona*) had similarly become the main part of the revenue and the heaviest burden on the taxpayer.

The combined effect of frequent devastation and looting, both by Roman armies and by barbarian hordes, and of wholesale requisitioning of crops and cattle, both for meat and for transport, was disastrous to agriculture, the basic industry of the Roman Empire. Peasants deserted their holdings, either drifting to the towns, where they could pick up a living in luxury trades ministering to the rich – for landlords still collected their rents – or becoming outlaws and brigands; large hordes of these ravaged Gaul in the latter years of the third century, and under the name of Bacaudae, and even proclaimed their own emperors. The government endeavoured to supply the shortage of agriculture labour by distributing barbarian prisoners of war to landowners, but by the reign of Aurelian the problem of 'abandoned lands', which was to harass the imperial government for centuries to come, was already affecting the revenue, and the emperor ruled that town councils were collectively responsible for deficits in taxation arising from that cause within their territories.

Devastation, requisitions and the shrinkage in the cultivated area led inevitably to frequent famines, and epidemics ravaged the under-nourished population. It is very difficult to estimate the effect of these losses, combined with war casualties, on the population, especially as we have no evidence whatsoever on the birth rate. But it may well be that the population of the Empire, which seems during the first and second centuries, and indeed in the first part of the third, to have been slowly expanding, received a setback and, temporarily at any rate, shrank during the latter part of the third century.

Concurrently with the wars and economic dislocation, and due partly to them, partly to more deep-seated causes, there occurred a general unsettlement of the traditional order of society. This order had, in the second century, been based on a series of hereditary but not rigidly closed classes, which by tradition and custom performed certain functions in the administration, defence and economic life of the Empire. At the top of the senatorial order was legally an hereditary caste, though naturally some families died out, and the emperors from time to time promoted into it deserving officials of the equestrian order and provincial notables: it was the function of senators to hold the ancient republican offices and to govern the provinces and command the armies. The equestrian order, which supplied officers to the army and officials to the civil service, was not legally hereditary, and access to it was, in fact, freely given to persons with the requisite property qualification, whether their fathers had held this rank or not; but the son of an equestrian official, unless he passed into the senate, normally succeeded to his father's rank.

Decurions, or town councillors, were again not legally an hereditary class, but, in fact, some councils were close corporations which co-opted the sons of members, and rarely admitted a commoner, even though he had acquired the necessary amount of property. The position of a town councillor was financially burdensome, since he was expected by law or custom to subscribe generously to the needs of the town, particularly when he held a municipal office. It was, in fact, largely through the munificence of decurions that the magnificent games and festivals of the cities were celebrated and the grandiose public buildings were erected which still impress visitors to southern France, North Africa and Syria. The position also involved a heavy burden of work and responsibility, since the council not only managed municipal affairs, but carried out for the central government many functions, such as the collection of the tribute and of requisitions and the maintenance of the imperial postal service and the repair of imperial roads. Nevertheless, the old tradition of civic patriotism survived, and service on the town council was, if not coveted as a prize, loyally undertaken as an honourable duty.

In the lower orders of society the army relied upon voluntary enlistment. Many recruits were drawn from the peasantry of the frontier provinces, but a large number were sons of veterans. In the lower grades of the civil service the officials were either soldiers, seconded for special duty, or slaves or freedmen of the emperor, who were normally succeeded by their sons, born in servitude. The peasants, though legally the majority of them were tenants on short leases, in practice cultivated the same plot from generation to generation.

This traditional order of things was profoundly shaken by the troubles of the third century. At one end of the scale peasants began deserting their holdings, either moving to another landlord who offered better terms, or abandoning agriculture altogether for the towns or for a career of banditry. The sons of veterans tended not to enter the army, but preferred to live as gentlemen of leisure on the proceeds of their fathers' discharge gratuities, which usually took the form of land or were invested in land. At the other end of the scale, a large number of senatorial families were killed off or reduced to poverty by the executions and confiscations which often followed a change of emperor, and their places were filled by new men. Senators began to evade the traditional magistracies, which were extremely expensive, and to be excluded from the government of the more important provinces, and in particular from the command of armies, by the policy of the emperors, who preferred to entrust such responsible posts to their own friends, who they hoped would not rebel. The equestrian order was thrown open to the lower ranks of the army, who could now aspire to become officers, governors of provinces and commanders of armies, and finally be acclaimed emperors. In the middle class, both because the burdens of office had increased and the old tradition of civic loyalty was dying, decurions strove to evade municipal office, and sons of decurions election to the council. The populace still got their games, but building ceased, and the huge monuments erected by past generations began to fall into disrepair. What was more serious, the whole administrative system was threatened with breakdown, since it was by the voluntary services of the landed gentry that the imperial taxes were collected. The government insisted that offices must be filled and the council kept up to strength, and ruled that a candidate duly nominated must accept office unless he could prove a claim to exemption.

On all sides the old traditions and the old loyalties were fading. At no time had the Roman Empire inspired any active devotion in the great majority of its citizens. Men were proud to be Roman citizens and not barbarians, but were not moved by loyalty to Rome to sacrifice their lives or their money. The Empire was too vast and impersonal and the emperor too distant to excite any emotion except respectful fear or sometimes gratitude. The loyalties on which the empire depended were local or professional. The soldier fought for the honour of his legion or his army or his general; the decurion worked and spent his money freely for the greater glory of his town. The generals and administrators of the senatorial and equestrian orders were moved rather by the traditions of their class than by devotion to the Empire. Now the sense of *noblesse oblige* was fading among the aristocracy, the spirit of civic patriotism was fast vanishing in the middle class, the discipline of the troops was decaying, and there was nothing to take their place.

On 20 November 284, there was yet another pronunciamento. The emperor Numerian, who had been leading back the legions from an expedition against Persia, was found dead in his litter, and the officers elected and the troops acclaimed the commander of the bodyguard, Valerius Diocles, or, as he was henceforth called, Diocletian. In the following spring he marched westwards, and defeated Numerian's brother, Carinus.

These events doubtless created little stir at the time: the Roman world was only too used to proclamations of emperors and civil wars. But they were to prove the beginning of better days. Diocletian was to reign for over twenty years, and then to abdicate of his own free will in favour of successors of his own choosing, and during these twenty years he was to carry out a thorough reorganization of the Empire, which in its main outlines was to last for three centuries.

The new emperor was, if a persistent later tradition is to be believed, of even humbler origin than his predecessors. His father was reputed to have been a freedman of a senator, and to have earned his living as a clerk. Diocletian himself must have shown some military ability to have risen to the post of commander of the bodyguard. But he was not a distinguished soldier, and when he had achieved power usually preferred to delegate the command in important operations to others. His genius lay in organization: he had a passion for order and method, which at times degenerated into a rigid insistence on uniformity, and an enormous capacity for work and an attention to detail, which are attested alike by the scores of constitutions issued by him and preserved in the Code, and by the thorough remodelling of the administrative, military and financial institutions of the Empire which he achieved. But his true greatness lay in his willingness to delegate authority, and in the absolute loyalty which he won from the colleagues whom he selected. He must have possessed a truly dominating personality to drive his team, for, as events after his abdication were to prove, the men of his choice were no ciphers, but men of ambitious and vigorous, not to say violent, character.

Only a year after his defeat of Carinus, Diocletian decided that he needed an assistant to deal with the problems of the West, in particular the peasant revolt of the Bacaudae in Gaul, and on 1 March 286, he nominated an officer of Illyrian origin and peasant birth, Maximian, as Caesar, or subordinate emperor, and at the same time adopted him as his son: he had no son of his own, a fact which simplified his problems. About six months later, faced by the proclamation of a rebel Augustus in Britain, Carausius, he promoted Maximian to the rank of augustus: henceforth Diocletian and Maximian were constitutionally co-ordinate, but Diocletian remained the senior Augustus, and in fact completely dominated his colleagues. This relationship was expressed by the surnames of Jovius and Herculius which they now assumed: Diocletian was the vice-regent upon earth of Jupiter, the king of the gods, Maximian of Hercules, the hero who under his father Jupiter's guidance had toiled for the benefit of mankind.

Seven years later Diocletian decided that two Augusti were not enough to control all the armies and deal with all the perils which beset the Empire. On 1 March 293 two Caesars were created, one to serve under Diocletian in the East, the other under Maximian in the West. For the former post Diocletian selected Galerius Maximianus, the son of a Dacian father and a barbarian mother, an energetic but brutal soldier, and married him to his daughter Valeria. As the other Caesar, Maximian chose Flavius Constantius, marrying him to his stepdaughter, Theodora. Constantine's mother, Helena, was divorced, and disappears from view for over thirty years. Constantine himself was sent off to the court of Diocletian, doubtless as a hostage for his father's good behaviour. It was probably at this date that there was painted at Maximian's palace at Aquileia a family group of the Augustus and his Caesar and their families, in which Maximian's little daughter Fausta was depicted offering a helmet, almost too heavy for her to carry, to the little boy Constantine.

Constantine was not to see his father again, till twelve years later he returned to stand beside his death-bed. During that time Constantius abundantly justified his choice. He reconquered Britain from the usurper Allectus, Carausius' successor, and in a series of campaigns he beat back the German tribes who had encroached on the Rhine frontier.

This done, he set about restoring the ruined cities of Britain and Gaul. We possess a glowing speech of thanks delivered in 298 on behalf of Autun, which had been wrecked in the peasant revolt of the Bacaudae. The orator was a certain Eumenius, who had been one of Constantius' secretaries of state, and had on his retirement been appointed professor of literature at Autun. Eumenius describes how Constantius not only supplied funds from the treasury for rebuilding the temples and public buildings and even private houses, but imported building workers from Britain and lent the city military labour from the legions. The Caesar, he declares, took a particular interest in education, and in testimony of this he quotes his own letter of appointment, which, as the only document dictated – or at any rate signed – by Constantine's father, is worth quoting.

Our Gauls deserve that we should wish to provide for their sons, who are instructed in the liberal arts in the town of Autun, and so also do the young men themselves, who with unanimous alacrity joined my train when I returned from Italy. What other reward ought we to confer upon them than that which Fortune cannot give or take away? We have therefore thought it most appropriate to appoint to this chair, which is vacant by the death of the professor, you, whose eloquence and moral character is well known to us from the performance of your official duties. Accordingly, without prejudice to the privileges of your office, we urge you to return to academic life, and in the aforesaid city, which, as you know, we are restoring to its former splendour, to educate and improve the minds of the young ; and we beg you not to think that in taking this post you in any way diminish the honours which you have previously won, for an honourable profession adorns rather than derogates from high rank. Finally, we wish you to receive from municipal funds a salary of 600,000 *nummi*, that you may understand that our clemency has had regard for your merits also.

During these years Constantius and his second wife produced a large family of half-brothers and half-sisters for Constantine. There were three daughters: Constantia, whom Constantine was to marry to his colleague and rival Licinius, whom he defeated and killed in 324; Anastasia, whom he was to give to Bassianus, the Caesar whom he nominated in 314, only to disgrace and execute him forthwith; and Eutropia, who alone seems to have enjoyed a quiet married life with Nepotianus, an undistinguished senator who became consul in 336. Of the three sons one, Hannibalianus, seems to have died young. Another, Flavius Delmatius, was in the last decade of Constantine's reign to hold office as censor, and his two sons, Delmatius and Hannibalianus, were to be raised to be Caesar and King of Armenia respectively, only to be lynched by the troops after Constantine's death. Constantine's other half-brother, Julius Constantius, preferred a life of retirement: his only title to fame is that he was the father of two sons, the Caesar Gallus and Julian the Apostate.

For the next twelve years Constantine was to be a member of that strange institution, the 'sacred retinue', the migratory capital of the Empire. Diocletian was perpetually on the move, inspecting the frontiers, reviewing the administration of the provinces and suppressing occasional revolts. It so happens that during the years after Constantine joined his train we can reconstruct his itinerary with some exactness from the subscriptions to the constitutions which he issued *en route*.

Constantine probably joined the court at Sirmium (Mitroviça on the Sava), where Diocletian had spent the winter of 292/3. But by 1 April the court was at Heraclea, on the Sea of Marmora, and on the 2nd at Byzantium. On the 15th it was moving westward again, and on the 17th it reached Heraclea once more, then went on to Hadrianople (Edirne, 10 May), Beroe (Stara Zagora, 17 May), Philippopolis (Plovdiv, 25 May), Serdica (Sofia, 24 June) and so back to Sirmium. Here Diocletian stopped for a year, but on 8 September 294 he was on the move again. During the next two months he was marching down the Danube from Singidunum (Belgrade) to Durostorum (Silistra), thence southwards to the Black Sea coast at Marcianopolis (near Varna), and past Anchialus and Deultum, both near Burgaz) to Hadrianople, and from here westwards to Hereclea and Byzantium. He crossed the straits on 10 or 11 November, and proceeded to Nicomedia (Izmit), his favourite residence, where he spent the winter. By next May he was

in Damascus, and in the following year he was summoned
to Egypt by the rebellion of Domitius Domitianus. After
an eight months' siege Alexandria fell in the summer of
297, and that same summer Diocletian was recalled to
Syria by news of a Persian invasion. He summoned his
Caesar, Galerius, to whom he had entrusted the Danube
frontier, to bring up reinforcements and conduct the campaign. After an initial defeat Galerius won a decisive
victory at Nisibis, and Diocletian signed the most advantage-
ous treaty Rome had ever made with Persia. The Great
King resigned his claims on Armenia, to whose throne its
pro-Roman refugee monarch, Tiridates, was restored, and
furthermore surrendered a number of satrapies beyond the
Tigris. During the next few years Diocletian is found at
Damascus, but in 302 he revisited Egypt. It must have been
on one of his marches through Palestine to or from Egypt
(that is in 296, 297 or 302) that Eusebius, a priest of Caesarea, first saw his future hero by Diocletian's side, 'having
already passed from childhood into adolescence'.

Apart from the crack regiments like the Lancers, who
accompanied the emperor on his march, the host of officials who followed in his train must have formed a veritable
army, and one can imagine the horror of the municipal
magistrates when the advance party of the court arrived
and proceeded to requisition all the best houses in the
town as offices and billets, and to demand the instant
production of incredible quantities of corn, meat, game,
oil and wine. In towns where the emperor normally resided for any length of time, he usually built a palace, reserved for his own use, but no such provision was made for
his officials. So strong was the force of habit that, for many
years after the court had settled permanently at Constantinople, officials still occupied billets; the rule was by then
that the unwilling host might retain two thirds of his house
for his own use.

The emperor's personal household was under the charge of an official appropriately named the camp commandant, who controlled a large staff of orderlies, cooks, waiters and so forth; the inner sanctum of the 'sacred bedchamber' was attended by a corps of eunuchs, who, despite their servile birth and barbarian origin, were persons of some political consequence, since they controlled access to the emperor. The emperor's person was guarded by a corps of officer cadets, selected from the ranks of the army and destined after service on the staff to be promoted tribunes of units. Closely attached to the emperor were the secretariats, under the control of the Master of the Sacred Memory, apparently a private secretary; the Master of Studies, who seems to have controlled the registries and archives; the Masters of Latin and Greek Letters, who drafted outgoing correspondence in the two languages, and the Master of Petitions, who prepared rescripts in answer to complaints and requests from subjects. The personnel of the secretariats was controlled by an establishment officer, the Tribune and Master of the Offices, who also had charge of the offices which arranged audiences with the emperor and organized his itinerary, and of a body of interpreters to deal with foreign envoys. The Master of the Offices also controlled the corps of imperial messengers, who carried proclamations, edicts and dispatches to the provinces. To supervise them a number of senior messengers were stationed in each province as inspectors. The whole corps was greatly hated and feared by the public and the local officials, since it was popularly – and rightly – believed that they, and particularly their inspectors, were used as a secret police by the central government. Quite separate from the imperial secretariats, which dealt mainly with routine matters, and of higher rank, since it handled confidential matters of state, was the secretariat of the imperial privy council, now called the consistory, because the members, high officials and others nominated for their legal knowledge or political, administrative or military experience no longer sat in the emperor's presence, but stood. This secretariat was drawn from the officers of the praetorian guard: the 'praetorian tribunes and notaries' were often employed on confidential state missions in the provinces.

Two finance ministries likewise followed the emperor on his travels. The first, under the Master of the Imperial Accounts, controlled the old cash taxes, the most important of which were by now the customs and the free-will offerings and crown money, the mints and the mines which supplied them with metal, the imperial wardrobe, and cash disbursements, mainly periodical donations. A hundred years later the establishment of this ministry was 449 secretaries, clerks and artificers (to provide master dies for the mints), grouped in eighteen departments. The second ministry, under the Master of the Imperial Private Property, handled the vast complex of real property which had in the course of centuries accrued to the emperors by bequest, escheat or confiscation, and collected new estates which fell in constantly. The revenue arising from this source was not regarded as a Civil List, but spent for ordinary public purposes.

These palatine ministries were almost rivalled by the giant department of the emperor's prime minister, the Praetorian Prefect. The Praetorian Prefecture was at this period at the summit of its long and curious development. The Prefect no longer, it is true, had effective control of the praetorian guard, which was permanently stationed at Rome; but he was by compensation the emperor's chief of staff and adjutant-general, often taking command of a field army, and controlling discipline throughout the forces and organizing recruitment. He was also Master-General of the Ordanance, having under his charge the state armament factories which Diocletian established in many

cities of the empire, and Quartermaster General, responsible
for supplying uniforms and rations to the entire army and
civil service. Thus, owing to the fact that requisitions and
payments in kind had become the most important part of
imperial revenue and expenditure, the Prefect had developed
into the principal finance minister, far overshadowing
the old masters of the Imperial Accounts and Private
Property. He also controlled the imperial post, a vast chain
of posting stations strung out along all trunk roads, which
supplied not only horses and carriages for travelling
officials and others favoured with an imperial warrant,
but also teams of oxen and heavy wagons for conveying
government stores of all kinds, ranging from bullion and
coin to textiles, foodstuffs, building stone and timber. Furthermore, the Praetorian Prefect was a supreme judge, co-
ordinate with the emperor, who accepted no appeals from
his court, with a jurisdiction – mainly appellate – extending to all cases, civil and criminal. Finally, since the Prefect
was, through his military, financial and judical duties, in
constant touch with the provincial administrations, he
acquired a general control over them, and was the normal
channel whereby the emperor communicated his instructions to provincial governors.

During the years that Constantine was at court, Diocletian was steadily remodelling administration, defence
and finance. On the administrative side the chief weakness
lay in the lowest stratum of the structure, where it was
becoming more and more difficult to goad town councils
into performing their functions. Diocletian did much to
keep the councils up to strength, and it was probably in
his reign that the doctrine became established that sons of
decurions were legally bound to enter the council. Even
so, every election of a magistrate or collector on the council produced a crop of appeals to the provincial governor,
and arrears in requisitions had frequently to be exacted

by his officials. In the larger provinces it became impossible for the governor to keep pace with the work.

To remedy this situation Diocletian reduced provinces to a manageable and more or less uniform size – some huge old provinces were subdivided into four or five – and carved Italy, hitherto officially under the senate, into provinces. In order to relieve the central government from the increasing burden of routine administrative work, he created a new unit, the diocese, between the province and the centre. The diocese was controlled by a deputy praetorian prefect, responsible for the same services as his chief, and also had an accountant, and an intendant of imperial domains, who answered to the Masters for their respective departments. The twelve dioceses were substantial areas: Britain, Gaul (northern France with the Rhineland and Low Countries), Viennensis (southern France), Spain (including Portugal and Morocco), Italy (including Sicily, Sardinia and Corsica), Africa (Algeria, Tunisia and Tripolitania), Pannonia, Moesia and Thrace (the western, central and eastern Balkans), Asiana and Pontica (south-western and north-eastern Asia Minor) and the Orient (Cilicia, Syria, Palestine and Egypt with Cyrenaica).

In military affairs Diocletian's chief work was to raise the strength of the army. In view of the greatly increased pressure of the barbarians this was essential if the frontier was to be held. According to his bitter critic Lactantius, Diocletian more than quadrupled the armed forces. This is an obvious exaggeration, but a study of the later army list of the Roman Empire suggests that Diocletian may have heavily doubled their numbers. It is significant that voluntary recruitment ceased to provide a sufficient intake. Diocletian had to make the military service of the sons of veterans compulsory, and to introduce a new system of conscription from the rural population of all the provinces. To ensure regular supplies of arms and uniforms, Diocletian established in numerous towns armament factories and wool- and linen-weaving establishments, the former manned by soldier artificers, the latter by slaves and convicts.

In strategy Diocletian was conservative. He held to the old system of a continuous line of defence strung out along the frontiers, reinforcing it with fresh units, building new forts and linking them with additional roads: in the deserts of Syria and North Africa his roads can still be traced and his forts still stand. For emergencies the regiments of the retinue provided a nucleus of a field army, but they had to be supplemented by drafts from the frontiers for any serious war. The command of the armies was separated from the civil government in many of the frontier provinces, and was entrusted to area commanders (*duces*), each responsible for a given length of frontier.

Diocletian attempted a reform of the currency, issuing gold coins weighing 1/60 lb. and genuine silver coins of 1/96 lb. But he continued to mint silverwashed copper and plain copper pieces in great profusion, and the inflationary movement gathered momentum. His famous edict of 301, in which he fixed prices and wages in the minutest detail, though enforced at first with ruthless severity, merely drove goods off the market, and had to be allowed to lapse. But in finance in the wider sense Diocletian carried out a reform of capital importance. The requisitions in kind (*indictiones*), which now formed the bulk of the revenue, had hitherto been levied in haphazard fashion, when and where required, and their incidence had been most inequitable. Diocletian consolidated them into one annual indiction, which was levied at a more or less uniform rate throughout the Empire. His first step was to hold a series of regional censuses, which were not actually completed until after his abdication. In these the land was surveyed and assessed in units of equal taxable value.

In Syria, where Diocletian himself was in charge, the assessment was very complex and accurate, the land being valued at different rates according to its agricultural use – pasture, arable, vineyard, olives – and to its quality in each category; the unit of assessment, the *iugum*, consisted of varying quantities of land which came to the same total value. Elsewhere the assessment was more rough and ready: in Africa the unit was the *centuria*, a fixed area of land without regard to its use or quality. The rural population and the animals were also counted and assessed in *capita*. Here again there were local variations. In some areas every adult counted as one *caput*, in others only males were counted, in others women were reckoned at half rate; animals were assessed at various fractions of a *caput*.

The land of every proprietor was thus assessed in uniform fiscal units, usually called *iuga*, and its population, human and animal, in uniform *capita*.

Henceforth it was possible, by a simple multiplication sum, to calculate the yield from a given city, province or diocese, or from the whole Empire, of a levy at any given rate on every *caput* or *iugum* it contained, and the Roman Empire for the first time could have an annual budget, the indiction, calculated to meet estimated expenditure. The system was applied to levies of all kinds, not only money and food crops, but uniforms, horses for the cavalry, beasts for the postal system and recruits for the army. Diocletian seems to have made separate levies of money on *capita* and of supplies on *iuga*. Under his successors a final simplification was introduced. *Iuga* and *capita* were equated for fiscal purposes, and levies were assessed on the total number of *iuga* and *capita* for which each estate was assessed.

Diocletian was gradually bringing order out of chaos, but the price was heavy.

He made three partners of his realm, dividing the empire into four parts and multiplying the armies, while each of them aspired to have a far larger number of troops than earlier emperors had had when they governed alone. The numbers of those who received began to be larger than the number of those who gave, so much so that the resources of the peasants were exhausted by outrageous levies. The fields were deserted and arable turned into forest. And to fill every place with terror, the provinces were chopped into fragments. There were more governors and more officials to watch over individual districts and almost individual cities, not to speak of hosts of accountants and controllers and deputies of the prefects, all of whom were little occupied with civil actions, but with constant condemnations and confiscations, frequent, or I should rather say continual, exactions of innumerable kinds, and intolerable brutalities in these exactions. Equally intolerable were the methods used in levying recruits. With insatiable avarice he never allowed his treasuries to be depleted, but always piled up extraordinary resources for his expenditure, so that he could keep what he hoarded complete and untouched. When by his various iniquities he caused a huge rise in prices, he tried to enact a law fixing the prices of goods offered for sale. Then much blood was shed on paltry and trifling charges, and nothing appeared on the market for fear, until inevitably, after many had died, the law was relaxed. To this was added an insatiable passion for building, and a corresponding exaction from the provinces, in producing labourers, craftsmen, wagons and everything needed for building works. Here he built a law court, there a race-course, here a mint, there an armament factory, here a palace for his wife, there one for his daughter.

Lactantius' prejudice is obvious, but there is more than a grain of truth in his criticisms. Diocletian could find no way to secure the defence of the frontiers save to increase the number of troops, and his efforts to make the creaking wheels of the administration revolve only resulted in more and more officials. There were coming to be more idle mouths than the primitive economic system of the Roman

Empire could feed. It is hard to remember that, despite its great achievements in law and administration, the splendid architecture of its cities and the luxurious standard of living of its aristocracy, the Roman Empire was, in its methods of production, in some ways more primitive than the early Middle Ages. Agriculture followed a wasteful two-field system of alternate crop and fallow. Yarn was spun by hand with a spindle, and textiles laboriously woven on clumsy hand looms. Even corn was ground in hand querns or at best in mills turned by oxen: windmills had not been invented and watermills were still rare. In these circumstances the feeding and clothing of an individual demanded a vast expenditure of human labour, and the maintenance of any substantial number of economically unproductive persons laid a heavy burden on the rest.

The result of the government's increasing demands for supplies was that the owners of land of marginal quality found that the levies exceeded the rent that they could extract from their tenants and abandoned their estates, and that the peasants who cultivated poor land had so little left after paying their taxes if they were freeholders, or the increased rents if they were tenants, that they could not feed their children. The population could not expand to meet the increased demand for soldiers and for workmen in the mills which supplied them. A chronic shortage of manpower ensued, and to safeguard essential industries the government froze the labour employed in them, compelling the workers to remain in their jobs and their children after them. It is difficult to trace the stages whereby labour in all industries essential to the state was gradually frozen, but in the key industry, agriculture, the peasant was probably already tied to his plot by Diocletian, by the ruling that where he was entered on the census registers there he must stay.

Diocletian was by tradition and temperament a conservative. Like all the emperors of the later third century, he claimed to be the restorer of the Roman world : he was not trying to shape a new order of society, but to press the rebellious forces of the age back into the old moulds. To make the old order work, he was obliged to introduce revolutionary changes, but his conservative, even reactionary, instincts are shown in such details as his insistence on dating by the Roman consuls. In religion, too, he was a conservative : he went back to the old Roman gods, choosing Jupiter Optimus Maximus as his patron rather than new deities, such as the Unconquered Sun to whom Aurelian had accorded the highest honour. On one religious problem, the treatment of Christians, there were two series of precedents which he might follow, and here he was to change his mind.

3   Paganism and Christianity

It is impossible to give coherent account of the paganism of the later Roman Empire, for it was not a coherent system. It was a strange amalgam of beliefs and cults from many lands and every stage of culture, ranging from a lofty if rather vague pantheism to the crudest animal worship. It was bound together only by mutual toleration, and indeed respect, and by a strong tendency to syncretism, whereby gods of different lands were identified one with another, and their myths woven together within the general framework of Greek mythology.

The official heads of the pantheon were the state gods of Rome, with whom had long been identified the Greek Olympians. But it may be doubted whether, outside Italy and Greece, their original homes, these gods gave much spiritual solace to their worshippers. The educated classes, it is true, the senatorial and official nobility, and the older and wealthier families of city councillors who formed the provincial aristocracy, had a deep-rooted sentimental attachment to them. They had been brought up on the Greek or Latin classics from childhood, and associated with the ancient gods their splendid heritage of art and literature and the glorious history of Greece and Rome. But apart from its literary and historical association, the official pantheon meant little to the later pagan world. The official worship of the emperors, dead and living, had even less religious content. No one really believed that the emperors were gods – no one, for instance, ever prayed to them in sickness or danger for health and safety. Their cult was merely the traditional mode of paying respect to the head of the state, usually a mere form, sometimes a vehicle for a genuine emotion of loyalty to the Empire. Most members of the educated aristocracy, while punctiliously performing the old-world ceremonies, and finding in them an aesthetic and nostalgic pleasure, found spiritual consolation either in philosophy or in one of the more emotional oriental cults.

Philosophy had by this time travelled far from its Greek starting-point. It was no longer inspired by intellectual curiosity, but had become fundamentally religious; in the philosophical textbooks of the day it was common to set forth the doctrine as a revelation by a divine sage, such as Hermes the Thrice Greatest, the Egyptian Thoth. The dominant schools of the age, Neoplatonism and Neopythagoreanism, were dualist systems of belief, which held that matter was evil, the body was a tomb, and that salvation lay in subduing the flesh and contemplating in the purity of the spirit the Godhead, the mysterious One of which the human intellect could predicate nothing. This philosophy was not incompatible with popular religion. The Supreme Godhead was generally conceived as manifesting himself in a series of emanations, and to the vulgar he revealed himself in allegories.

The attitude of the educated to the faith of the masses was thus one of rather condescending reverence. Even the most childish myths and the most beastly rites, not only of Greece and Rome, but of the lower cultures, were regarded as divinely inspired. To the wise, who could penetrate their inner meaning, they were allegorical representations of sublime truths; for the vulgar, who believed in them literally, they were the highest form of the divine truth to which their souls, blinded by the fog of the material world, could attain. Nor was philosophy incompatible with a belief in astrology and magic. The universe moved in one great harmony, and the courses of the sun and the moon and the stars were all part of the same vast movement as the lives of men. The wise man, who had broken free of the trammels of this material universe, could, by his spiritual powers, overcome mere material obstacles: most of the famous philosophers of the day were reputed to be wonder-workers.

At the bottom end of the scale a welter of local cults received the devotion of the peasantry and of the bulk of the urban proletariat, particularly in the smaller cities, whose character was predominantly rural. The Egyptians worshipped their beast-headed gods, and the sacred animals were venerated during their life and on their death solemnly embalmed. In the huge temples multitudes of shaven priests in white linen robes officiated in age-old rituals in an ancient language which they dimly understood. In Syria and in Punic North Africa the villagers and townspeople worshipped a multitude of local Baals and Ashtoreths with fertility rites which shocked Christian ideas of sexual morality. The ritual prostitution at Heliopolis, and more particularly at Apheca, whose river ran red each year with the blood of the slaughtered Adonis, was later to justify Constantine in closing these two great temples. Farther north lay Emesa, where men worshipped the stone that the Sun God had sent down from heaven, and Doliche, the centre of another meteoric cult, which the legions had carried westwards to the Balkans. In Asia Minor the dominant figures, under a bewildering variety of names, Cybele of Pessinus, Ma of Comana, Artemis of Ephesus, were the Great Mother and her youthful son and consort, in whose honour their frenzied worshippers castrated themselves. Among the Thracians, mounted warrior gods were worshipped, and farther west in Illyricum the

Unconquered Sun was the chief object of devotion. In Celtic lands nature-worship prevailed, and reverence was paid to gods and goddesses of the springs and rivers and forests, and above all to the sun.

By the mass of the peasants and townsmen their gods were conceived as local potentates, the protectors of their village or town. The nomes of Egypt each had their own patron deities, with their appropriate sacred animals, and savage brawls were common, when the inhabitants of a nome which venerated Souchos and regarded crocodiles as sacred killed a hippopotamus, the totem of a neighbouring nome. Even a god or goddess who was worshipped over a wide area was often qualified by a local adjective, and possessed a separate local personality. Many-breasted Artemis of the Ephesians, though she was equated with the Artemis of Greek mythology, was the peculiar patroness of Ephesus, and Ephesians abroad would pay their reverence to her, rather than to the local Artemis. But among the more cultured classes local gods were freely identified, often on the slenderest grounds, with figures of the Greek and Roman pantheon, and on inscriptions the local deity is more often than not disguised as Zeus or Jupiter, Aphrodite, Venus or Hercules. In this way the multitudinous and diverse cults of the Empire were bound up into some loose semblance of unity. In some more cultivated circles this process of syncretism was carried to its logical conclusion, and all gods and goddesses were regarded as local manifestations, either of the particular god or divine group which they favoured, or, if they were philosophically inclined, of the Ineffable One.

Between the philosophic pantheism of the aristocracy and the local cults of the masses stood the mystery religions. Their appeal lay particularly to the cosmopolitan population of the larger towns, slaves and freedmen who had been cut off from their native cults, traders and merchants and seamen who spent their lives travelling from place to place; and also in the cosmopolitan atmosphere of the army and the civil service, where men from diverse countries mingled. Their main clientele was thus the urban middle and lower classes. They penetrated hardly at all to the rural areas, the villages and small towns, whose inhabitants were for the most part satisfied with their traditional local gods. On the other hand, they made a considerable appeal to the aristocracy, who were no longer emotionally satisfied with the official pantheon, and did not all find an adequate solace in philosophy.

One of the distinctive features of these cults was, as the name given to them implies, that they were secret. Their rites and their theology were only revealed to initiates, often gradually by successive stages of initiation. Another was their interest in a future life: they all, with more or less vagueness, assured to their initiates bliss in some world beyond the grave. All again attempted in some degree to allay the sense of sin. They offered purification, primarily by taboos and ritual acts, although most included some moral teaching. All again were of oriental origin, and owed much of their success to their exotic flavour and to the glamour of ancient learning popularly attributed to the immemorial East.

The oldest-established of these cults in the West was the worship of the Great Mother of Pessinus and her consort Attis. The black stone which was her fetish, accompanied by her Phrygian eunuch priests, had been solemnly conveyed from Pessinus to Rome on the order of the Sibylline books in the dark days of the Second Punic War when the official Roman cults had failed to allay popular alarm and despondency. The senate had, however, been somewhat dismayed by the barbaric and orgiastic character of her ritual, and strictly secluded her worship to her temple on the Palatine; the devotion of the Roman people was given in the western form of annual chariot races. In the reign of Claudius, however, this seclusion was broken, and the worship of the Great Mother began to spread among the populace both of Rome and of the Italian and provincial towns, where it enjoyed a certain prestige above other oriental cults in virtue of its official approbation by the Roman state.

We can reconstruct with some accuracy the ritual of its great spring festival. It opened on 15 March with a procession of the Reed Bearers, which probably commemorated the discovery by the goddess of Attis, who had, like Moses, been exposed on the reedy banks of a river, the Phrygian Sangarius. This day was marked by the sacrifice of a bull. There followed a week of fasting. Then the pine tree which symbolized Attis was cut and decked and a day of mourning followed. The next day, 24 March, was the Day of Blood, when the devotees of the goddess, working themselves up into a religious frenzy by music and dance, slashed themselves with knives and finally castrated themselves with a flint. A night of watching followed, and on the 25th the resurrection of Attis was celebrated with joyous festivities. Finally, after a day of rest, the statue of the goddess was carried in solemn procession to be bathed in the sea. So much the vulgar crowd saw. For those who wished to penetrate deeper into the inner meaning of the rites, there was a sacramental meal, where the worshippers 'ate from the drum, and drank from the cymbal, and became initiate of Attis'.

A later arrival in the Latin West, at first banned by the Roman government, but given official recognition by Caligula, was Isis, with her consort Serapis and their son Horus. The cult was a conflation of Greek and Egyptian elements. The art form of the representations of the Triad in purely human guise, the bearded father, and the mother and child, was Greek. On the other hand, the temples of Isis were built in a more or less Egyptian style, and the priests were vested in the Egyptian manner and made music with the sistrum. The liturgy seems to have been conducted in Greek, but reproduced the daily ritual routine of the Egyptian temples – the opening of the shrine at dawn, the washing and vesting of the god, and so on to the closing of the shrine at sunset. The principal festival of the year occurred in the autumn, and symbolized in dramatic form the myth of the death and dismemberment of Serapis by Typhos, the search by Isis for the fragments of the body and the resurrection of Serapis. The inner meaning of these rites and myths was revealed only by stages to worshippers, who had to pass through three degrees of initiation.

The third and most recent cult was that of the Persian Mithras, which, for long domiciled in eastern Asia Minor, seems first to have migrated westwards late in the first century A.D. Mithras was a god of heavenly light, often identified with the sun, the champion of justice and truth against the dark powers of evil. The chief incident of his career, which is the subject of the majority of Mithraic sculptures, was the slaughter of the bull, from whose body arose all vegetable and animal life useful to man. The faithful passed through seven grades of initiation, becoming in turn Ravens, Bridesmen, Soldiers, Lions, Persians, Runners of the Sun and Fathers. The rites, which were celebrated in caves or crypts, included a sacramental meal of bread and wine, and the *taurobolium*, wherein the worshipper, crouching in a cavity in the floor, was literally washed in the blood of a bull, slaughtered on a grating above, thus acquiring the vital force of the bull whom Mithras had slain for the benefit of mankind. This rite became very popular and was also associated with the cult of the Great Mother.

Some general characteristics of the age require underlining. It was in the first place an intensely religious period.

Except among a small coterie of Epicureans, rationalism or scepticism was non-existent. Everyone, from the most highly educated intellectual to the most ignorant peasant and worker, believed intensely in the power of supernatural forces and their interest in human affairs. Men believed that good or ill-fortune depended on the unseen, and sought, according to their temperament and belief, to divine the inevitable future, to constrain the supernatural by magic, to placate the anger of the gods or win their favour, or enter into a communion with the divine which would place them beyond the reach of earthly troubles.

In the second place, the religion of the age was to a great degree other-worldly and escapist. Despairing of true happiness for themselves in this life or of the triumph of peace, justice and prosperity on earth, men turned their thoughts to a future life beyond the grave or to a spiritual life detached from the material world. In the mystery religions, as has been pointed out above, the dominant motif was to seek assurance for a life after death. As Attis was slain and rose again, so those who gained mystic communion with him and learned his secrets would live in blessedness after their earthly death. As Osiris was torn in pieces and brought to life, so those who were instructed in the ancient lore of Egypt would know the password to the world beyond. Souls purified by his mysteries Mithras would escort through the seven planetary spheres to the highest heaven, where they would live for ever in eternal light. In philosophical circles there was a strong tendency to regard the material world as inherently evil, and the body 'a cloak of darkness, a web of ignorance, a prop of evil, a bond of corruption, living death, a conscious corpse, a portable tomb'. Its adepts sought release from the evils of this world in contemplation of and communion with the Ineffable One.

This is not to say that either religion or philosophy gave

no practical moral teaching. The philosophers taught that the soul must be purged of carnal appetites and passions by the practice of virtue in order to attain the purity requisite for contemplating the divine. The doctrine of Mithraism was that the universe was a battleground of the forces of Light and Darkness, Evil and Good, and that worshippers of Mithras must join his fight to attain union with him. In the cult of Isis, too, moral purity was demanded from her worshippers, if they were to hope to be acquitted in the judgement beyond the grave and achieve eternal bliss. Morality was, however, save perhaps in the Mithraic system, regarded as the concern of the individual, a means of purifying his soul and gaining for it full illumination or future blessedness. Neither philosophy nor religion took any interest in social justice, or had any hope or even desire of remedying the evils of the world.

Paganism was scarcely at all organized, and to a very large extent lacked a professional priesthood. Cults were maintained by the Roman state, by cities, by villages and by private societies. The Roman state conducted through its magistrates and official priests the worship of the Roman gods. It also exercised a police jurisdiction over all cults, regulating or banning those which it considered inimical to the material, moral or spiritual interests of the empire. But beyond this negative, and very lax, control, the central government did not interfere. The majority of local cults were maintained by the cities of the empire, who appointed their priests and financed them either from the municipal revenues or from special sacred funds and endowments. Villages similarly often had their own temples of priests. The mystery cults were congregational in character. A body of worshippers formed a club, choosing their own priest, and paying for the expenses of worship by subscription.

A full-time professional priesthood existed in Egypt. It

was an hereditary body, and its recruitment was regulated by an official of the Roman government, who scrutinized the pedigree and physical fitness of entrants, and examined them in their knowledge of hieroglyphics. He also inspected the temples to ensure that the cult was properly conducted and that the priests devoted the whole of their time to their sacred duties and observed the rules of their order as to shaving their heads and wearing linen garments. It is probable that in the empire-wide cult of Isis, the priesthood was full-time and professional, since the elaborate daily ritual could not otherwise have been maintained, but there is nothing to show that the priests belonged to the Egyptian sacred caste. It is possible that other oriental temples were served by professional priests, and that oriental cults which spread to the West, such as Mithraism, required the full-time services of a regular clergy. But even in widespread cults like those of Isis and of Mithras there was no central authority which laid down doctrine, regulated ritual or authorized the appointment of priests. In the great majority of local cults the priesthoods were filled by local worthies, who combined or alternated their sacred duties with other public offices. Most priests were elected by the local council, either, like most offices, for a year, or, as a special honour, for life: some priesthoods, which carried with them the enjoyment of considerable revenues, were sold by auction; a few were hereditary in the family of the founder of the cult.

Inchoate and unorganized though it was, paganism was very pervasive. Religion was intimately interwoven with public and social life. Sessions of the senate at Rome began with the burning of incense on the altar of Victory, and it is probable that the meetings of city councils opened with some religious service. Magistrates were expected in the course of their duties to make sacrifices to the gods on behalf of their city and to take part in religious processions and celebrations. Practically all public entertainments were festivals in honour of the gods, and theatrical shows, athletic competitions and chariot races were opened with prayers and sacrifices. All education was based on the study of the ancient poets, and the very themes for composition were drawn from pagan mythology.

Christianity in many ways resembled the mystery religions. The Christians had their Saviour God, who had died and risen again. They had their degrees of initiation into his mysteries, and they had their secret sacramental meal, in which the inner circle of initiates entered into communion with him: like the other cults, they organized themselves in congregations, maintaining their priests by subscription. The religion, moreover, appealed to the same social strata as the other mystery cults, to the urban middle and lower classes: it, too, hardly touched the rural masses. With the upper classes it had made less headway than the other mystery cults.

But it had one great difference from the other cults. Its adherents refused to worship the other gods, and even abhorred them as demons. Hence they tended to be exclusive and clannish. They would not attend public festivals or athletic sports or theatrical shows. They even made difficulties about dining out, since most of the meat in the shops had been sacrificed to idols. They avoided joining the army, either because they might, in the course of their military duties, have to attend pagan worship, or because as soldiers of the Lord they could not give their allegiance to a power which they sometimes equated with the Prince of Darkness. For similar reasons their richer members refused to hold office in the cities or sit on the council and subscribe to the needs of the town.

Driven in upon themselves, the Christian communities developed a very strong corporate spirit and a closely knit though flexible organization. The congregation of each

city and its priests and deacons were ruled with absolute
authority by a bishop, chosen for life by a rather complicated procedure, which combined approval by the clergy
and laity of the town with the assent of neighbouring
bishops, one of whom at least had to confer upon the candidate his charismatic grace. The congregations of the
various cities had always kept in close touch by correspondence, and it gradually became customary to settle
differences of doctrine and discipline by conferences of
bishops.

From the beginning the Christians were, like the Jews
whom they so much resembled, disliked by their pagan
neighbours. They were denounced as atheists, accused of
being traitors to the Empire, but above all they were hated
as peculiar people, who did not join in the social life of
their neighbours but kept themselves to themselves. And
since they were disliked, they were popularly believed to
indulge in sexual promiscuity at their secret 'love feasts'
and practise horrible rites of infant sacrifice. Did not their
holy books enjoin upon them to 'eat the flesh of the Son
of Man and drink his blood'?

Unlike the Jews, the Christians very early, and for
reasons which are obscure, incurred the hostility of the
imperial government. The two cults had very similar ob-
jectionable features, but in the eyes of the Roman government there was one vital difference. The Jews were a race
who practised the traditional worship of their ancestors,
and had at an early date, while still a political unit, obtained from Rome legal recognition for their peculiar practices. With their great respect for ancestral custom and
legal precedent, the Romans therefore tolerated and even
privileged Jews. Christians, on the other hand, were inno-
vators, starting a new cult which, on the face of it, being
devoted to a criminal duly executed by a Roman governor,
was undesirable. The government disliked new cults in

general as being liable to cause civil disturbances and only too often to introduce immoral practices, and this particular cult was always occasioning riots and lay under grave suspicion of immorality. Whatever the reason, as early as the beginning of the second century Christians who after due warning persisted in their cult were liable to the death penalty.

At first, however, the imperial government took no active steps against the new cult. It was left to informers to denounce Christians, and repressive measures were only sporadically and locally applied, usually under pressure from popular opinion; for the governing classes were in the first two centuries mainly agnostic, or at any rate did not take religion very seriously. But as during the latter years of the third century religiosity increased in all classes, and as uneducated men of strong religious conviction rose from the lower ranks of society to high administrative or military posts, and to the purple itself, the temper of the government changed. The civil wars and barbarian invasions, the famines and plagues, were surely a sign that the gods were angry with the empire. And it was not difficult to discern the reason for their anger: the number of atheists who refused them worship was steadily growing.

It was the emperor Decius who in 250 made the first systematic attempt to enforce the universal worship of the gods and thus to extirpate Christianity. By his orders all inhabitants of the empire had to sacrifice to the gods before the authorities and obtain certificates that they had done so. The apparent success of this measure was spectacular: thousands of Christians, particularly those in the upper classes who could less easily evade the order, submitted. But very many went into hiding, and a substantial number defied the government, braving imprisonment, torture and death. The courage of the confessors and martyrs roused the enthusiasm of the Christians and impressed the pagans, and, so soon as the persecution waned, those who had lapsed petitioned the bishops to be readmitted. Seven years later the emperor Valerian renewed the attack on other lines, ordering the arrest of members of the senatorial and equestrian orders and imperial freedmen who refused to sacrifice, and first deporting and later executing all bishops and priests, and forbidding religious meetings. But Valerian was soon afterwards taken prisoner by the Persians, and his son Gallienus not only released the clergy, but restored their buildings and cemeteries to the churches. For the next forty years the Church enjoyed almost uninterrupted peace. Converts flowed in, and in the great cities large churches were built on prominent sites. The old exclusiveness began to break down. We know of one Christian conscientious objector who refused to serve when called up under Diocletian's conscription, and of two or three serving soldiers who refused obedience on grounds of conscience; but the proconsul who dealt with the first case pointed out to the young conscript that there were many Christian soldiers in the imperial forces. As Christianity percolated into the upper ranks of society, the objections to holding office began to fade, and a council of Spanish bishops, on the eve of the Great Persecution, ruled on what conditions Christians might hold municipal offices and the provincial high priesthood of the imperial cult – an indication of how secular this cult had become. Christians became provincial governors, and were even to be found occupying high positions at the imperial court. And as Christian exclusiveness broke down, pagan prejudice began to wane: in the last persecutions it was the government that was the moving force, and the public seems to have been apathetic, and even on occasion disgusted with the violence of the authorities.

It was during this period, too, that the Church com-

pleted its organization. It became the established practice
for the bishops of a province to meet regularly in its capital city or metropolis. The bishop of the capital, the metropolitan, who presided at this meeting, thus acquired a
certain precedence and claimed authority over his
neighbours. Certain great cities acquired a more extensive
primacy. The authority of the bishop of Carthage was
recognized in all the Latin-speaking provinces of Africa from
Mauretania to Tripolitania; that of the bishop of Antioch
from Cilicia and Mesopotamia in the north to Palestine in
the south. The bishop of Alexandria enjoyed exceptional
powers throughout Egypt and Cyrenaica, nominating
every bishop in the country. Rome exercised a similar
jurisdiction over the suburbicarian diocese of southern
Italy and the islands; it had long, whether as the capital
of the Empire or the see of Peter, enjoyed an undefined
primacy throughout the Roman world.

4   The Great Persecution

It was probably in 298 that an incident occurred which was to bring misery to thousands. Diocletian and his caesar Galerius were sacrificing to obtain omens – no doubt for the Persian war – but when the soothsayers examined the victims' livers they could discover none of the usual markings: fresh victims were sacrificed, but again without success. At length Tagis, the chief soothsayer, declared that the sacrifice did not work because profane persons were present. It emerged that some of the officials present were Christians, and had been defending themselves from the demons by crossing themselves. Diocletian was furious, and ordered that all members of the court should sacrifice on pain of flogging; an order was also sent out throughout the Empire that soldiers and civil servants should sacrifice or be discharged.

The Church did not take very seriously the dismissal of its members from the civil service and the army; they were probably not very numerous. But worse things were in store. We do not know what went on within the imperial palace at Nicomedia, though Lactantius, an African Christian who had been appointed professor of Latin literature at Nicomedia by Diocletian, professes to reveal to us the inner secrets of the imperial council. It would seem that Diocletian, who had for nearly twenty years pursued a policy of toleration, was reluctant to take any further steps, but that the pace was forced by his caesar Galerius, a rabid pagan, son of a barbarian priestess. The oracles were asked for their guidance, and Constantine in later years told the story of Apollo's response:

They said that Apollo then proclaimed from some cavern or dim hole – and not from human lips – that the just upon the earth prevented his speaking the truth and that was the reason why the oracles from his tripod were false. This evil among men did his priestess lament with dishevelled locks and frenzied motions. But let us see how it ended. I call upon thee now, Highest God: I then heard, when I still was quite a child, how he who at that time held first rank among the emperors of Rome, an unhappy, a truly unhappy man, his soul deceived by error, idly asked his bodyguard who were the just upon earth, and one of the priests who attended him said in reply, 'The Christians, of course.'

Constantine, on any reckoning, must have been by now in his teens, that is by Roman ideas no longer a 'child', but his error is more intelligible if he had been fifteen than if he had been twenty-five.

On 23 February 303 there was posted an edict at Nicomedia ordering that all copies of the scriptures should be surrendered and burned and that all churches should be dismantled, and prohibiting meetings for Christian worship. A party of troops forthwith marched out and demolished the great church of the capital, which stood in full view of the palace. Next day a supplementary edict went up depriving all Christians of any official rank which they possessed, thus making them liable to torture, and debarring them from bringing actions in the courts; imperial freedmen were to be reduced to slavery. A bold Christian tore down this edict and was put to death after prolonged torture.

Soon after, a fire broke out in the palace. The Christians were accused of attempting thus to compass the death of the emperors, their bishop was executed, and Christian

members of the imperial household – three eunuchs are
mentioned – were tortured to obtain information and finally executed. A fortnight later another fire broke out in
the palace, and revolts were reported from Melitene and
Syria. As a counter-measure a second edict went out, ordering the arrest of all bishops and priests.

During this summer Diocletian travelled westwards to
visit Rome, perhaps for the first time in his long reign, there
to celebrate his Vicennalia, the twentieth anniversary (as
the Romans reckoned it) of his accession, on 20 November 303. He left Rome on 18 December, was at Ravenna
on 1 January, and spent the greater part of 304 on the
Danube frontier, returning to Nicomedia to conclude the
celebration of his twentieth year by dedicating a new race-
course. He was already in bad health when he arrived, and
soon was very seriously ill. On 13 December his life was
despaired, but on 1 March 305 he reappeared in public, so
emaciated as to be scarcely recognizable.

Meanwhile, the arrest of the clergy was causing the government embarrassment; for the city gaols were not intended for long-term imprisonment – a penalty unknown
to Roman law – but merely to hold malefactors pending
trial. It was decided to take advantage of the amnesty cus-
tomarily granted on festal occasions to release them on the
Vicennalia, but to avoid losing face the government ruled
that before being released they must sacrifice, and a third
edict went out to this effect. The local authorities evidently received instructions that by hook or by crook the
clergy must all be made to submit. Some gave in after
threats or beating or torture, others were physically constrained to go through the motions of sacrifice, others were
issued with certificates though they had resisted to the last.
A few contumacious recusants were excluded from the
amnesty and later executed: two died at Caesarea, and
one at Antioch on 17 November. In the spring of 304 a

fourth edict was promulgated ordering everyone to sacrifice.

The first edict was promulgated throughout the Empire,
but in Britain and Gaul it was not fully enforced by Constantine's father, who dismantled or demolished the churches, but did not insist on the surrender of the scriptures;
he is said not to have inflicted the death penalty. In Maximian's dioceses it was enforced without such scruples. At
Thibiuca, in Africa, the edict was posted on 5 June, and as
the bishop, Felix, was away, the mayor ordered Aper his
priest to be summoned: he declared that the bishop had
the scriptures and professed ignorance of his whereabouts,
and was placed under arrest. Next day the bishop appeared,
and the following dialogue ensued:

The Mayor: 'You are Felix, the bishop?'
The Bishop: 'Yes.'
The Mayor: 'Give up any books or papers that you have.'
The Bishop: 'I have some, but I will not give them up.'
The Mayor: 'Give up the books so that they can be burned.'
The Bishop: 'It would be better for me to be burned than the
divine scriptures; for it is better to obey God than man.'
The Mayor: 'The orders of the emperors are more important
than your talk.'
The Bishop: 'The command of the Lord is more important
than that of men.'
The Mayor: 'Think it over for three days, because if you
neglect to perform what has been ordered here in your own
city, you will go to the proconsul and will continue this con-
versation in his court.'

Felix still refused after his remand, and was sent to
Carthage on 14 June. On 15 July, after imprisonment and
interrogation by the proconsul's legate and the proconsul
himself had failed to shake his determination, he was beheaded.

At Abitinae, another little African town, a priest, Saturninus, was discovered by the local authorities holding a religious service in a private house: he and his congregation, forty-eight men, women and children, were arrested and sent to Carthage. Here they were examined under torture to obtain their confessions of having broken the imperial order. The prisoners made no attempt to deny their guilt, but confessed more than they were asked. The proconsul is examining Saturninus' son of the same name:

The Proconsul: 'And were you present, Saturninus?'

Saturninus: 'I am a Christian.'

The Proconsul: 'That was not my question, but whether you attended a religious service.'

Saturninus: 'I attended service because Christ is the Saviour.'

The proconsul now turned to the elder Saturninus.

The Proconsul: 'What is your confession, Saturninus? Look in what a position you are placed. Have you any scriptures?'

Saturninus: 'I am a Christian.'

The Proconsul: 'I am asking you whether you held a religious meeting and whether you have any scriptures.'

Saturninus: 'I am a Christian. There is no other name which we ought to venerate after Christ.'

The Proconsul: 'Since you persist in your obstinacy, you must confess under torture whether you have any scriptures. Torture him.'

Young Saturninus now burst out: 'I have the scriptures of the Lord, but in my heart. I pray thee, Christ, give me strength to endure. My hope is in thee.'

The Proconsul: 'Why did you disobey the order?'

Saturninus: 'Because I am a Christian.'

Against these heroic actions, drawn from the Acts of the Martyrs, may be set the prosaic official record of what happened at Cirta, the modern Constantine in Algeria: 'In the eighth and seventh consulships of Diocletian and Maximian,

19 May, from the records of Munatius Felix, high priest of the province for life, mayor of the colony of Cirta. Arrived at the house where the Christians used to meet, the Mayor said to Paul the bishop: "Bring out the writings of the law and anything else you have here, according to the order, so that you may obey the command."'

The Bishop: 'The readers have the scriptures, but we will give what we have here.'

The Mayor: 'Point out the readers or send for them.'

The Bishop: 'You all know them.'

The Mayor: 'We do not know them.'

The Bishop: 'The municipal office knows them, that is, the clerks Edusius and Junius.'

The Mayor: 'Leaving over the matter of the readers, whom the office will point out, produce what you have.'

Then follows an inventory of the church plate and other property, including large stores of male and female clothes and shoes, produced in the presence of the clergy, who include three priests, two deacons, and four subdeacons, all named, and a number of 'diggers'.

The Mayor: 'Bring out what you have.'

Silvanus and Carosus [*two of the subdeacons*]: 'We have thrown out everything that was here.'

The Mayor: 'Your answer is entered on the record.'

After some empty cupboards had been found in the library, Silvanus then produced a silver box and a silver lamp, which he said he had found behind a barrel.

Victor [*the Mayor's clerk*]: 'You would have been a dead man if you hadn't found them.'

The Mayor: 'Look more carefully, in case there is anything left here.'

Silvanus: 'There is nothing left. We have thrown everything out.'

And when the dining-room was opened, there were found four bins and six barrels.

The Mayor: 'Bring out the scriptures that you have so that we can obey the orders and command of the emperors.'

Catullinus (another subdeacon) produced one very large volume.

The Mayor: 'Why have you given one volume only? Produce the scriptures that you have.'

Marcuclius and Catullinus [*two subdeacons*]: 'We haven't any more, because we are subdeacons; the readers have the books.'

The Mayor: 'Show me the readers.'

Marcuclius and Catullinus: 'We don't know where they live.'

The Mayor: 'If you don't know where they live, tell me their names.'

Marcuclius and Catullinus: 'We are not traitors: here we are, order us to be killed.'

The Mayor: 'Put them under arrest.'

They apparently weakened so far as to reveal one reader, for the Mayor now moved on to the house of Eugenius, who produced four books.

The Mayor now turned on the other two subdeacons, Silvanus and Carosus:

The Mayor: 'Show me the other readers.'

Silvanus and Carosus: 'The Bishop has already said that Edusius and Junius the clerks know them all: they will show you the way to their houses.'

Edusius and Junius: 'We will show them, sir.'

The Mayor went on to visit the six remaining readers. Four produced their books without demur. One declared he had none, and the Mayor was content with entering his statement on the record. The last was out, but his wife produced his books; the Mayor had the house searched by the public slave to make sure that none had been overlooked. This task over, he addressed the subdeacons: 'If there has been any omission, the responsibility is yours.'

This little narrative is probably typical of what happened in most places. We see the mayor meticulously carrying out his orders, keeping his temper admirably on the whole in the face of the obstructive attitude of the clergy, content to have their declarations entered on his record if they alleged they had nothing to produce. We see the pitiful evasions of the clergy, reluctant to give away their colleagues directly, but willing to tell the authorities where they can find the necessary information.

In the dioceses subject to Diocletian and Galerius we have record of only two arrests under the first edict. At Heraclea, in Thrace, the church was, on receipt of the edict, merely locked and sealed, and it was not till later that the provincial governor, observing the bishop, Philip, holding a service outside it, put him under arrest with his priest and confiscated the church plate and scriptures. In Palestine, Procopius, a reader of Scythopolis, was arrested on entering Caesarea – he was presumably wanted for copies of the scriptures. The governor, exceeding his orders, demanded that he should sacrifice to the gods, or at any rate make a libation to the emperors. Procopius replied with the Homeric verse: 'A multitude of lords is not good. Let there be one lord, one king.' For his seditious reflection on the régime of the four emperors, he was executed on 7 June.

There is no evidence that the second and third edicts were ever promulgated in the dominions of Maximian and his Caesar: they were perhaps regarded as precautionary police measures against the local attempts at arson and revolt in the eastern dioceses. More curiously there is no sound evidence for the promulgation of the fourth edict in the West, where *traditio*, or surrender of the scriptures, was to be in later years a burning question, whereas *thurificatio*, or sacrifice to the gods, completely overshadowed this question in the East. In the East we have more or less authentic records of several martyrdoms in various provinces, but full statistics for Palestine only, where Eusebius kept an accurate record. Here, after one execution under the first edict and two under the third, there was one under the fourth. Later six young men provoked their own fate by presenting themselves before the governor with their hands bound behind their backs, shouting that they were Christians. They with two others who had been previously arrested and tortured were all beheaded on 24 March 305, about a year after the edict was issued. We cannot tell how far Palestine was typical of the eastern provinces generally. In Phrygia there was one horrible incident, where a little town which was Christian to a man was burnt over its inhabitants' heads; and in Egypt, where Christianity was widely spread among the fanatical peasantry, Eusebius declares that while he was there large numbers were beheaded or burned on one day. Nor is the number of executions a fair test of the misery inflicted. The government was not out to kill, but to secure submission, and hundreds and even thousands of Christians underwent prolonged imprisonment, being tortured and remanded time and time again, without ever suffering the supreme penalty. It was usually for deliberate acts of contumacy that death sentences were inflicted.

On 1 May 305, before a large parade of troops at Nicomedia, Diocletian abdicated, and on the same day his colleague, Maximian, resigned the purple in the West. Their Caesars were proclaimed Augusti, Galerius taking over the dioceses of Moesia, Thrace, Asiana and Pontica, Constantius adding Spain to his existing diocese of Britain Gaul and Viennensis. Two new Caesars were nominated, both soldiers of peasant origin, Severus to rule Pannonia, Italy and Africa, Maximin to govern the great Oriental diocese.

The motives which lay behind this dramatic move we can only conjecture, though Lactantius once again

professes to take us behind the curtains of the palace, and
reproduces the threats of Galerius and the feeble protests
of Diocletian. It cannot have been long premeditated, or a
more obvious date, such as the completion of the emperor's
twentieth year of rule, would have been chosen. Probably
Diocletian really wanted rest after his serious illness, and it
may be that, regarding his illness as possibly divine vengeance from the Christian God, he wished to take no further responsibility for the persecution. Having made this
decision, he naturally compelled his colleague, Maximian,
to follow suit – much against his will, as later events
proved – in order to prevent heartburning between the two
Caesars. In the choice of the new Caesars Lactantius again
professes to take us behind the scenes. The natural choice,
according to him, would have been Maxentius, Maximian's
son, and Constantine, Constantius' son, but Diocletian rejected the former as unfit and Galerius refused the second,
and insisted on the nomination of two creatures of his
own. In point of fact, it is likely that both Diocletian and
Galerius, having no sons, disapproved of the hereditary
principle, and not only was Maxentius a worthless young
man, but Constantine was far too young. He had, it is true,
been promoted tribune – probably prematurely because he
was his father's son – and had seen a little active service on
the Danube, but he had no experience. In reality Galerius,
no doubt, had a considerable say in the nomination of his
own Caesar, Maximin, but there is no sound evidence that
Severus was his nominee; Maximian, it is true, later backed
his son against him, but only to regain power himself.

Constantius, now senior Augustus, requested Galerius to
send his son to him: he was ailing and wished to see him
before he died. Galerius, suspecting that there would be a
coup d'état if young Constantine were on the scene when
his father died, made excuses and kept putting him off. At
length one morning he yielded and signed Constantine's

travel warrant. Lactantius tells the dramatic sequel. Galerius' habit was, after dispatching official business in the morning, to dine well: his praetorian prefect had standing orders to ignore all postprandial commands. Next morning he repented of his weakness in allowing Constantine to go, and ordered him to be summoned. But he was nowhere to be found, and it emerged that he had at once started the previous afternoon. A party was dispatched to pursue him, but, arriving at the first posting station, found all the horses hamstrung. Having obtained other horses after infuriating delays, they pressed on to the next station, to find all the horses disabled there too. So Constantine got clean away.

He found his father at Boulogne, preparing to cross to Britain for a campaign against the Picts. The campaign over, Constantius returned to York, and here, on 25 July 306, he died. On the same day the army of Britain acclaimed Constantine Augustus.

Young Constantine – he was probably not much over twenty – thus early demonstrated two of his dominant characteristics; a craving for power, which was not to be satisfied till he was master of the whole Roman world; and a capacity for decisive action, which was to win him every war in which he engaged. From the circumstances of his upbringing his education had been scrappy, and his involved and bombastic style betrays the muddled thinking of a semi-educated man. By temperament he was authoritarian, generous to a fault, explosive of temper, but easily mollified. In his crude fashion he was strongly religious – he believed, that is, that success depended on the favour of higher powers.

Constantine was forthwith recognized in Britain and Gaul: Spain, which had only been subject to his father for little over a year, rejected his title. He hastened to regularize his position by sending his portrait, wreathed in bay, to Galerius, now the senior Augustus, thus asking for recognition. Galerius was furious at the usurpation, but he thought it best to accept the *fait accompli* and proclaimed Constantine, not as Augustus, but as Caesar; Severus, the senior Caesar, was at the same time proclaimed junior Augustus. Constantine accepted the lesser honour for the time being.

Three months later Galerius received another shock. Severus had been conducting a census in Italy and even in Rome itself, and this measure had caused unrest amid a population which had for centuries lived tax free. Then he announced the disbandment of the praetorian guard. A mutiny followed: Abellius, an unpopular official, was lynched, and on 28 October 306 the troops proclaimed Maxentius, the son of the retired Augustus Maximian. Maxentius also tried to secure Galerius' recognition, modestly entitling himself 'unconquered prince' on his coins meanwhile. But in this case Galerius was adamant: there was no room for a third Caesar in the imperial system, and he moreover personally detested his son-in-law. Severus was ordered to crush him, and early next spring he marched south from Milan. In face of this peril Maxentius, who had meanwhile rallied Africa and Spain and assumed the title of Augustus, called upon his father to help him proclaiming him Augustus for the second time. Maximian's name worked wonders, not only with Maxentius' troops, but with Severus', who deserted *en masse*, and Severus was forced to throw himself into the fortress of Ravenna, where, after a brief siege, he surrendered on the promise that his life should be spared.

Galerius now prepared to move against the usurper himself. Severus was promptly executed, and Maximian left for Gaul to seek Constantine's alliance. The bribe he offered was the hand of his daughter, Fausta, and the title of Augustus. It was a difficult moment for Constantine: he had been recognized as Caesar by Galerius, who was undoubtedly the legitimate senior Augustus; but he knew that his recognition had been grudgingly accorded and might well be revoked. Maximian, though his resumption of authority was illegitimate, had been lawful Augustus, and, moreover, looked like being successful in his pretensions. Constantine decided to accept his offer; but he took no action against Galerius.

The marriage of Constantine and Fausta was celebrated on 31 March 307, Constantine having first divorced his wife Minervina, by whom he already had a son, Crispus. We possess the speech delivered by a Gallic orator at the wedding-feast. The speaker lauds the valour of the young Augustus, who had already slaughtered thousands of Franks, and had thrown two of their captive kings to the beasts in the amphitheatre. He boldly chides Maximian for having ever laid aside his imperial power, and pictures Rome herself piteously pleading that he grasp the tiller once more. He plays much on the contrast in age between the two Augusti, Constantine, 'the adolescent emperor', who was, nevertheless, so mature in judgement, and the aged Maximian, still so full of martial vigour. And he prays for a long succession of Herculean monarchs as the fruit of the marriage.

Galerius was as unsuccessful as Severus. He advanced within a few miles of Rome, but becoming doubtful of the loyalty of his troops, beat a hasty retreat, ravaging the sacred soil of Italy to prevent his foes from following him up. Constantine no doubt congratulated himself on the choice he had made. But next spring he was faced with another choice. Maxentius, having made use of his father's name, did not propose to share his power with him. Maximian, indignant at his scurvy conduct, denounced him before an assembly of the troops, and tore his purple robe from him. But the troops supported the younger and more generous Augustus, and Maximian sought refuge with his new son-in-law in Gaul. Constantine had to decide between quarrelling with Maxentius, now the *de facto* ruler of Italy, Africa and Spain, or disowning Maximian, to whom he owed his title of Augustus. He decided to welcome Maximian, and accorded him every honour, but not the power after which the old man hankered. Shortly afterwards Africa, aggrieved by Maxentius' extortionate demands for money and corn, revolted, proclaiming as Augustus its deputy-prefect, an aged Phrygian named Domitius Alexander.

In the autumn of this year, 308, Galerius appealed to the aged Diocletian, who was living in retirement at Salona, to come forward and clear up the confusion, and on 11 November a conference was held at Carnuntum, attended by Diocletian, Maximian and Galerius. Diocletian refused to reassume the purple, and persuaded his old colleague Maximian to retire once more. To succeed Severus, Galerius nominated as junior Augustus Licinius, an old companion in arms, assigning to him the diocese of Pannonia till he should recover the areas usurped by Maxentius. Maximin continued as Caesar of the Oriental diocese, and Constantine was still, despite his presumption in assuming the title of Augustus, recognized as Caesar of Gaul and Britain. Maxentius and Alexander were ignored as usurpers.

Maximin not unnaturally resented Licinius being promoted over his head, and demanded from Galerius the title of Augustus. Galerius endeavoured to compromise by granting both him and Constantine the style of 'sons of the Augusti', but neither would accept this, and next spring Galerius had to acquiesce in Maximin's assumption of the title of Augustus, and at the same time to admit Constantine's claim to the same style. There were thus now four Augusti, Galerius, Licinius, Constantine and Maximin, who recognized one another, and two, Maxentius and Alexander, who were recognized by none but themselves. At about this time the diocese of Spain revolted from Maxentius, and acknowledged the authority of Constantine. Constantine had every reason to be satisfied: within three years he had gained for himself the position which his father occupied at his death, legitimate Augustus of Britain, Gaul and Spain.

After his official recognition by Galerius, old Maximian was no longer an asset to Constantine, but rather an embarrassment. The old man must have realized that there was no further prospect of his being called to power by his son-in-law, and he may have feared that he would be put out of the way. In the spring of 310, taking advantage of Constantine's absence on a campaign against the Bructeri, a German tribe who occupied the east bank of the Rhine opposite Cologne, he made a last bid for power. Giving out that Constantine was dead, he assumed the purple at Arles, seized the treasury, made a lavish donation to the garrison and sent dispatches summoning the troops at other stations. But he had underestimated his adversary's vigour and the loyalty of his troops. Directly the news was received at Cologne, the men clamoured to be on the march, refusing even to wait to receive money to purchase their supplies *en route*. With incredible speed they reached Chalons, where ships had been collected to carry them down the Saône and the Rhône, and, impatient with the slow speed of the barges, they insisted on rowing them down the stream. Before he had mustered his forces, Maximian heard that Constantine was upon him, and fled to Marseilles. Constantine pursued and at once attempted an assault on the walls. His ladders proved too short, but the troops within the city promptly opened the gates, and Maximian surrendered and was stripped of the purple. Soon afterwards he perished. Lactantius, writing some years later, tells a melodramatic story of his end. According to him, Maximian, ungrateful for having been spared his life, plotted to murder his son-in-law, endeavouring to persuade his daughter, Fausta, to leave her bedchamber weakly guarded. Fausta pretended to agree, but informed Constantine, who substituted for himself in the Emperor's bed 'a worthless eunuch who was to die in the Emperor's stead'; Lactantius apparently sees nothing immoral in the deliberate sacrifice of a slave's life. During the night Maximian entered, having informed the few guards whom he met that he had had an interesting dream which he wished to tell to his son-in-law, and drawing a dagger, stabbed the supposed emperor to the heart. As he emerged from the room, proclaiming his achievement, Constantine met him with a troop of soldiers. Convicted red-handed, he was given the choice of what death he would suffer, and hanged himself. But the orator who congratulated Constantine on the crushing of Maximian's revolt a few months after the event knew nothing of this. After describing the surrender of Marseilles, he says:

So as far as concerned your piety, Emperor, you saved both him and those whom he had deceived. Let him blame himself that he refused to accept your kindness, and did not think himself worthy of life, when he was permitted by you to live. You, and this should satisfy your conscience, spared even those that did not deserve it. But – pardon my words – you are not omnipotent : the gods avenge you even against your will.

From this it may be inferred the official version originally was that Maximian committed suicide in remorse, but that later it was deemed advisable to release a more circumstantial tale of treachery.

The same orator reveals the interesting fact which, as he remarks, had hitherto received surprisingly little publicity, that Constantine was descended from the emperor Claudius Gothicus. He elaborates at some length the superiority of the hereditary principle, pointing out that 'it was no chance agreement of men, no sudden outcome of popularity, that made you Emperor : you deserved the Empire by your birth'; and that, admirable though it be to earn power by valiant service in arms, as Constantine had done, it is the highest gift of the immortal gods to receive at birth what others scarcely attain by their whole life's labours. Constantine, he adds, has this advantage over his colleagues, that he is an emperor of such noble lineage that his office, which is his by right, without need for canvassing, adds nothing to his honour.

It has been suggested that this entirely fictitious claim to hereditary legitimacy was invented in order to fill the gap in his title caused by condemnation of Maximian's memory; for it might have been argued that, if Maximian was a tyrant, his creation of Constantine as Augustus was invalid. But now that Constantine had been recognized by Galerius, it was hardly necessary on that score, and if he did not wish to depend on his old enemy's grudging recognition, he could have based his claim on descent from Constantius, who had indisputably been senior Augustus. The claim was, in fact, far more ambitious, as the orator

delicately hints. It was that Constantine was the sole
legitimate emperor, since his hereditary claims went back
beyond the upstart Diocletian and all his creations.

Constantine had carried on his father's policy of toleration for the Christians. Lactantius indeed asserts that his
first act was 'to restore the Christians to their worship and
their God'; but he is presumably alluding to an edict confirming the existing situations. His personal devotion, if
we may judge by his coins, was to Mars, whom he styles
his father, preserver and champion, the giver of victory
and of peace. He also occasionally honours Hercules, his
official patron, and after he had put forward his claim to
descent from Claudius Gothicus, he shows special devotion to the Unconquered Sun, the favourite deity of his
putative ancestor – and of his father Constantius.

Maxentius also granted toleration to the Christians, and
later even restored its confiscated property to the Church
of Rome. In the East the situation was very different. Galerius and Maximin were both rabid pagans, and in their
dominions the persecution continued to rage. We know
most about Maximin's policy from Eusebius' detailed narrative of events in Palestine.

On his accession, on 1 May 305, Maximin allowed the
persecution to lapse for nearly a year. Then in the spring of
306 he issued an edict that everyone – men, women and
children – should sacrifice at the temples under the supervision of the magistrates of the cities: some attempt was
made to enforce this edict thoroughly, for we hear of military officers calling out names from a list. At Caesarea a
youth named Appianus rushed forward from the crowd
and tried to prevent Urbanus, the governor of Palestine,
from sacrificing: he was executed on 2 April. On the same
day another young man, Ulpianus, was put to death at
Tyre, and shortly afterwards Appianus' brother, Aedesius,
offered the same defiance and suffered the same fate at

Alexandria. The persecution soon waned, however, for when Maximin himself celebrated games at Caesarea on 20 November 306, only one Christian was thrown to the beasts, and he had been arrested under Diocletian.

Next year Maximin inaugurated a new policy: obstinate prisoners were no longer to be executed, but sent to hard labour in the mines and quarries, having first had their right eye blinded and the sinews of their left ankle severed. There were, however, still occasional executions – Theodosia, a girl of seventeen, on 2 April, and a man, Domninus, on 5 November. By the spring of 308, the quarries of Egypt could no longer hold the multitudes of Egyptian convicts, and ninety-seven were transferred to the copper-mines of Phaeno in southern Palestine. In the same year a number of Christians who had been holding secret services at Gaza were sent to the mines, and one of them, a woman, was tortured and executed for a seditious remark against the Emperor, together with another woman, who protested at her cruel treatment. On 25 July another execution followed, of a man named Paul; and shortly afterwards 130 more Egyptian convicts were transferred to Palestine and even farther north to Cilicia.

The same autumn Maximin decreed yet another general sacrifice, to be organized by provincial governors and mayors, magistrates and recorders of cities: moreover, all food in the markets was aspersed with libations, and sentries were stationed at the doors of the public baths to compel the bathers to sacrifice. At Caesarea three Christians emulated Appianus' exploit, and interrupted the governor of Palestine, now Firmilianus, as he was sacrificing: they were beheaded on 13 November, together with a woman named Ennathas. The pace now quickened: three Egyptians, carrying comforts to their brethren in the Cilician mines, were executed on 14 December, two Palestinians on 11 January 309, on 16 February a batch of twelve, including five Egyptians, returning from their errand of mercy in Cilicia, and two more on 5 and 7 March. After this the persecution died down, till in 310 the governor of Palestine inspected the mines at Phaeno. He found that supervision had been very lax, the convicts having even been permitted to build themselves churches. Four ringleaders, all Egyptians, were executed forthwith, and the remaining able-bodied prisoners were dispersed, some going to Cyprus, others to the Lebanon, others to different places in Palestine: thirty-nine, who had been excused work on the ground of age, ill-health and the mutilation they had suffered, were beheaded.

Galerius was as vigorous a persecutor as his junior colleague till, in the winter of 310-11, as he was preparing for the twentieth anniversary of his accession, he was stricken with a horrible disease, which seems, from Lactantius' gloating description of it, to have been cancer of the bowels. In his agonies he began to wonder whether it were not the God of the Christians, whose worshippers he had so ruthlessly pursued, that was avenging upon him the deaths of his followers. This conviction grew upon him, until on 30 April 311 he astounded his subjects by the following edict:

Among the other measures which we constantly take for the advantage and well-being of the commonwealth, we had previously wished, in accordance with the ancient laws and the public discipline of the Romans, to correct all abuses and to provide that the Christians also, who had abandoned the worship of their own fathers, should return to a sound mind; seeing that in some way such self-will had taken possession of these Christians and such folly had filled them, that they did not pursue the practices of antiquity, which their own ancestors had perhaps instituted, but, following their own will and fancy, made laws for themselves to observe and formed unions of different peoples in sundry places. However, when our command had gone out to the effect that they should return to the practices of antiquity, many were subdued by the threat, many also were thrown into panic. And when large numbers persisted in their purpose, and we saw that they neither paid due cult and reverence to the gods, nor worshipped the God of the Christians, in consideration of our most merciful clemency and regarding our consistent practice of granting pardon to all men, we thought fit in this instance to extend immediate pardon, that they may be Christians once more and may assemble their conventicles, provided they do nothing contrary to public order. We shall signify in another letter to provincial governors what rules they are to observe. Hence, in accordance with this our pardon, it will be their duty to pray to their God for our safety, and that of the commonwealth and their own, that the commonwealth may be made secure in every respect, and that they may be able to live free of trouble in their own homes.

A few days later Galerius died. Maximin promptly occupied his Asiatic and Licinius his European dominions; their troops faced one another across the straits, but war was averted. Throughout the Empire the Christians rejoiced over the recantation of the arch-persecutor and marvelled at the signal vengeance of God upon his enemy. Constantine may already have wondered whether the strange god whom the Christians worshipped was not a power to be feared.

Maximin thought it prudent to accept Galerius' edict, which had already been promulgated in his newly acquired dioceses of Pontica and Asiana. He did not publish it in his old diocese of the Orient, but he instructed his praetorian prefect Sabinus to circularize to provincial governors a letter to the same effect:

With the most earnest and devoted zeal, the divinity of our lords the most divine emperors long ago determined to bring the minds of all men into a holy and upright way of life, so that those who appeared to follow a practice alien to that of the Romans might pay due worship to the immortal gods. But the obstinacy and stubborn will of some went so far that neither would they, by proper respect for this command, withdraw from their own purpose, nor could the penalties inflicted terrify them. Since therefore it resulted in this way, that they subjected themselves to danger, in accordance with the nobility of their piety the divinity of our lords, the most mighty emperors, considering it alien from their own divine purpose to subject men to such danger for such a cause, has ordered that it be notified to your prudence through my devotion, that if any of the Christians be found following the worship of his people, you should free him from all molestation and danger, and should not consider anyone deserving of punishment on this count, since in the course of so long a time it has proved impossible to persuade them in any way to abandon such obstinacy. Your diligence should therefore write to the mayors, magistrates and rural police officers of the several cities, that they may know that they are not henceforth to pay any attention to this constitution.

The prisoners were forthwith released from the gaols and the convicts returned to their homes from the mines, cheered as they passed through the cities by jubilant crowds. The churches were reopened and thronged with joyous worshippers. The question of the lapsed was promptly submitted to a council of bishops, who assembled at Ancyra (Ankara), and the following rules were laid down. Priests and deacons who had sacrificed, but on being ordered to do so a second time had resisted, should retain their titles, though excluded from their functions: excepted from the benefit of this rule were those who, by a collusive arrangement with the officials, had obtained a bogus second test with no real torture. Those who had suffered loss of their property, torture or imprisonment, but had ultimately yielded to physical force and been made to go through the motions of sacrifice were declared guiltless. Among those who had submitted and attended a sacrificial feast, a distinction was drawn between those who had done so gaily in their best clothes, and those who had done so weeping and in mourning, and those who were bold enough to bring their own food with them to the feast. Severer penalties were ordained for those who had, even under constraint, sacrificed two or three times, those who had yielded to mere threats and had given no indication of repentance till the persecution was over, and those who had not merely lapsed themselves but betrayed their comrades.

But six months had not passed before Maximin, undeterred by his colleague's fate, began to renew the persecution. This time his attack was indirect, and on more intelligent and constructive lines. In the autumn of 311 the city council of Nicomedia petitioned him that no Christians should be allowed to live in their city or its territory. Maximin graciously acceded to this request, and other cities followed suit, including Antioch and Tyre: Eusebius has preserved the Emperor's lengthy and rhetorical reply to the Tyrians. Soon whole provinces were making the same requests; an inscription records the petition of the provincial council of Lycia and Pamphylia. At the same time Maximin sought to revivify the pagan cult by appointing a high priest for each city, to supervise the other priests and make daily sacrifice to all the gods, with authority to prohibit Christian worship, public or private, and arrest Christians and compel them to sacrifice, or hand them over to the provincial governors. Over these civic high priests were appointed provincial high priests of higher rank to direct and stimulate their activity. The whole scheme was modelled on the organization of the Church, with its bishops in each city controlling the priests, and the metropolitans of the provinces supervising the bishops, and it shows that Maximin was an intelligent man not ashamed of learning from his adversaries.

At the same time propaganda was organized against

Christianity. Spurious Acts of Pilate, which placed the founder of the sect in an opprobrious light, were posted up in all public places in town and country, and all schoolmasters were directed to teach them to their pupils. Some Damascene prostitutes were induced to make written confessions that they had been Christians and had taken part in the orgies of sexual promiscuity in which the Christians indulged at their Sunday meetings, and these confessions were also posted up everywhere.

Maximin at first maintained his earlier ruling that obstinate recusants were not to be executed but condemned to hard labour after mutilation. But by the autumn of 312 executions had begun again. At Emesa three citizens, including Silvanus, the bishop of the town, were thrown to the beasts. Lucian, a priest of Antioch and a famous theologian, was brought before Maximin at Nicomedia and executed. And on 24 November Peter, bishop of Alexandria, was beheaded with several other Egyptian bishops.

In the West, meanwhile, relations between Constantine and Maxentius had been becoming more and more strained. Now that his father had died at Constantine's hands, Maxentius suddenly became once more a pious son, issuing coins in honour of 'the divine Maximian, his father'. Even more impudently, he similarly honoured the divine Constantius, whom he claimed to be related to him by marriage and by blood: Constantius had, in fact, married his half-sister and was his brother by adoption. Maxentius thus implicitly laid claim to Constantine's dominions.

In the summer of 312 Maxentius strengthened his position by the reconquest of Africa. At about the same time Constantine sought to gain an ally by betrothing his half-sister, Constantia, to Licinius. Maximin, scenting in this combination a threat to himself, sent a secret embassy to Maxentius, and an alliance was formed.

It was Maxentius who formally declared war by the destruction of Constantine's statues and pictures in Rome and in the cities of Italy. He had, according to the pagan historian Zosimus, 170,000 infantry and 18,000 cavalry at his disposal, but after deducting the garrisons of Africa and Sardinia, Corsica and Sicily, he could not put much more than half this total in the line; even Constantine's panegyrists reckon the armies facing their hero at only 100,000 men. But Constantine's total forces amounted, according to Zosimus, only to 90,000 foot and 8,000 horse, and his panegyrists declared that he left more than three quarters of his forces to guard the Rhine frontier. Even allowing for exaggeration, he must have been outnumbered by over two to one.

According to Zosimus, Maxentius' plan was to invade Rhaetia and thus thrust a wedge between Constantine's and Licinius' dominions, and the disposition of his troops, the bulk of whom were concentrated at Verona, the gate to the Brenner Pass, supports this view. But whatever his plans were, they were not executed, for Constantine struck first. Crossing the Alps by the Mont Cenis, he descended to Susa. Here there was a small garrison, but Constantine's men set fire to the gates, scaled the walls by ladders and forthwith captured the town. Constantine wisely prevented them from plundering and had the fires extinguished, thus encouraging other cities to surrender.

Advancing towards Turin, he was met by a formidable army, including a large body of heavily mailed cavalry, *clibanarii*, an arm which the Romans had adopted from the Persians and was apparently unfamiliar to Gallic troops. Constantine, however, knew the correct tactics to deal with them. He instructed his men to yield to the solid wedge of armoured horsemen, and then, when their charge had lost its momentum, to close in on all sides and batter the riders with clubs. This manoeuvre was successful, and Constantine's men advanced and routed the remainder of their opponents, who fled *en masse* back to Turin, only to find that the citizens had closed the gates against them. A frightful slaughter ensued, after which Turin opened its gates to the victor. Milan now surrendered, and after pausing there for a few days Constantine passed on, routing the enemy's cavalry at Brescia, and arrived at Verona. Here was concentrated a large army under the command of Ruricius Pompeianus, Maxentius' praetorian prefect and an able and experienced soldier. His position, moreover, was extremely strong, since the town is surrounded on the north, east and south by the Adige, and the west side, facing Constantine, was protected by formidable fortifications. Constantine determined that he must cross the Adige in order to surround the city, and he found a ford some way upstream, over which he threw a force. Ruricius sent out a large detachment to mop up this party, but it was itself destroyed, and Constantine's men closed round the town. Ruricius slipped out to bring up reinforcements, and returned with a considerable army to raise the siege, but Constantine persisted in his assaults and met Ruricius with a small part of his forces only. A desperate encounter ensued, in which Constantine himself engaged. Ruricius was killed and his relieving army destroyed. Verona soon surrendered, yielding an embarrassing number of prisoners; the supply of handcuffs ran out, and more had to be hastily manufactured from the swords of the defeated army. Aquileia and Modena now surrendered, and the road to Rome was open.

Maxentius, as he was informed of the successive defeats of his armies in the north, appears to have decided to stand a siege in Rome. The great walls of Aurelian were considered impregnable, he had ample stocks of corn from Africa, and a large army, including his crack troops, the praetorian guards. As Constantine drew nearer, the populace grew restive, and at the chariot races which Maxentius celebrated on 26 October in honour of the forthcoming anniversary of his accession, 28 October, the crowd openly taunted him, shouting that Constantine was invincible. Maxentius was disturbed, and ordered the board of senators who had custody of the Sibylline Books to seek their guidance. They found in them a prophecy that on 28 October the enemy of the Romans would perish. Maxentius, who was superstitious, was impressed by this allusion to his accession day. He resolved to fight on his lucky day, and to make it luckier still, he forthwith appointed as prefect of the city the same man, Annius Anullinus, who had been prefect when he had been proclaimed.

On the fated day he marched out northwards, crossing the Tiber by the Milvian Bridge. Here the road divided: northwards ran the Cassian Way, north-eastwards, following the Tiber, the Flaminian Way. Maxentius chose the latter, which was the main north road; but when he had advanced a mile, at a place called the Red Rocks, where the road forms a defile between the hills on the left and the river on the right, he found his advance blocked by Constantine's men: their shields, he observed, bore a strange device: 'a letter "I" with its head twisted round and across it a letter "X"'. While he halted, debating whether to try to force the defile, a report came that Constantine's men, advancing along the Cassian Way, were attacking his men at the Milvian Bridge, and soon Maxentius' men found themselves hemmed in by the enemy, pressing in from the Cassian Way and forcing them back to the Tiber. The guards fought well, but the battle soon became a carnage. Thousands were drowned in the river, and a panic-stricken mob, amongst them Maxentius himself, struggled to force their way back over the bridge. As Maxentius was crossing, he was pushed over the edge. So the 'enemy of the Romans' perished.

Next day, 29 October 312, Constantine entered Rome

in triumph. Maxentius' body had been recovered from the mud of the Tiber, and his head was carried on a lance to convince people that he really was dead: later it was sent to Africa to announce to that diocese its change of masters. The senate obediently condemned the memory of the tyrant, and elected Constantine senior Augustus.

6   The Conversion of Constantine

That Constantine was in some sense converted to Christianity in the year 312 there is no manner of doubt. But at this point agreement ceases. The debate still goes on whether his conversion was a matter of policy or of religious conviction, and in the latter alternative what brought about his change of heart, and finally whether he became a full Christian or whether he passed through a stage when he regarded Christianity as one of many forms in which the Supreme Power could be worshipped. On the first question no historian who understands the mood of the age in which Constantine lived can entertain any serious doubts. To be a rationalist in that age Constantine would have been an intellectual prodigy, and he was, in fact, so far as we can discern him, a simple-minded man. And even if, by some freak of nature, he had been a sceptical freethinker, he would not on any rational calculation of his interest have chosen to profess Christianity. The Christians were a tiny minority of the population, and they belonged for the most part to the classes of the population who were politically and socially of least importance, the middle and lower classes of the towns. The senatorial aristocracy of Rome were pagan almost to a man; the higher grades of the civil service were mainly pagan; and above all the army officers and men, were predominantly pagan. The goodwill of the Christians was hardly worth gaining, and for what it was worth it could be gained by merely granting them toleration.

On the other questions there is doubt, for the evidence is tangled and in parts contradictory. It will be best first to set out the external facts – Constantine's actions, his official pronouncements and the public utterances of his contemporaries.

Long before the defeat of Maxentius, Constantine had favoured the Christians: he had granted them full toleration immediately upon his accession to power. But no ancient author claims that he was during that period a Christian, and the orators who from time to time delivered panegyrics before him had no hesitation in representing the pagan gods as his protectors. As late as July 311 Eumenius, in giving thanks for a remission of taxes on behalf of Autun, could say without offence, 'Our gods have created you emperor for our special benefit,' and compare Constantine's generosity with that of 'Earth, the author of crops, and Jupiter, the governor of the winds'.

Directly after the capture of Rome, Constantine went beyond toleration for the Christians. We possess three letters which he wrote during the winter of 312-13, one to Caecilian, bishop of Carthage, and two to Anullinus, proconsul of Africa. As the earliest evidence of Constantine's new attitude to the Church, they are worth quoting in full. The first runs:

Constantine Augustus to Caecilian, bishop of Carthage. Whereas I have decided that in all the provinces, the Africas, the Numidias and the Mauretanias, provision should be made for expenses to stated numbers of the servants of the lawful and most holy Catholic Church, I have written to Ursus, the accountant of Africa, instructing him to cause to be paid to your reverence 3,000 folles. You will therefore, upon receipt of the aforesaid sum, order the money to be distributed to all the previously mentioned persons in accordance with the list which has been sent to you by Hosius. If you discover that it is inadequate in order to fulfil my wishes in this matter towards all of them, you must without hesitation demand whatever you discover is needed from Heraclides, the intendant of our domains. For I have ordered him personally to cause to be paid without any delay any sums which your reverence may demand from him. And since I have heard that certain persons of turbulent character wish to distract the people of the most holy Catholic Church by some base pretence, you must know that I have given such orders personally to Anullinus the proconsul and also to Patricius, deputy of the prefects, that among all their other business they will devote especial attention to this matter, and will not submit to seeing anything of the kind happen. Accordingly, if you should observe any such persons persisting in their insane designs, approach the above-mentioned officials without any hesitation, and refer the matter to them, so that they may deal with them as I ordered them personally. May the divinity of the great God preserve you for many years.

By this letter Constantine embarks on a new policy of subsidizing the Christian Church from public funds; he no longer merely tolerates, but actively favours the Church. It is noteworthy, too, that he is already aware of the schism whereby the African Church was rent, and confines his favours to the side which he has been informed is the true Catholic Church. The source of his information is also revealed – the Spanish bishop, Hosius of Corduba. This is highly significant; for it suggests that Constantine had a Christian bishop at his court before he embarked on the Italian campaign.

Constantine's first letter to Anullinus runs as follows;

Greetings, our dearest Anullinus. It is the nature of our love of good that we are not merely not reluctant, but that we even wish to restore whatever belongs to others by right, dearest Anullinus. We therefore wish that when you receive this letter you shall immediately cause to be restored to the churches any of the property belonging to the Catholic Church of the Christians in the several cities or in other places, and now held either by private citizens or by any other persons. For we have decided that whatever the same churches previously held shall be restored to their ownership. Since therefore your devotion observes that the tenor of this our command is clear, take steps that gardens, houses, and all other property of the same churches are forthwith restored to them, so that we may hear that you have rendered the most careful obedience to this our command. Farewell, our dearest and most beloved Anullinus.

In this letter Constantine is merely righting the wrongs inflicted by the persecutions. The second is more significant.

Greetings, our dearest Anullinus. Whereas from many considerations it appears that the annulment of the worship in which the highest reverence of the most holy heavenly power is maintained has brought the greatest dangers upon the commonwealth, and the lawful revival and protection of this same worship has caused the greatest good fortune to the Roman name and exceptional prosperity to all the affairs of men, the divine beneficence affording this, it has been decided that those men who in due holiness and the observance of this law offer their personal services to the ministry of the divine worship shall receive the due reward of their labours, dearest Anullinus. Accordingly I desire that those who within the province entrusted to you provide personal service to this holy worship in the Catholic Church over which Caecilian presides, who are commonly called 'clerics', shall be kept immune from all public burdens of any kind whatever, so that they may not be diverted by any sacrilegious error or slip from the service which is owed to the Divinity, but may rather without any disturbance serve their own law, since their conduct of the greatest worship towards the Divinity will in my opinion bring immeasurable benefit to the commonwealth: Farewell, our dearest and most beloved Anullinus.

This letter reveals something quite new in Constantine's thought. The worship offered by the Christian Church to the Divinity is to his mind of vital importance to the well-being of the Empire; the persecution of the Church has brought the Empire into peril, its restoration and maintenance has brought it good fortune. It is clear that Constantine regarded Christianity not merely as a permissible and a laudable cult, but as the form of worship most acceptable to the supreme power in whose hands the destinies of the Empire lay.

In February 313 Constantine and Licinius met at Milan. The marriage of Licinius and Constantia, Constantine's half-sister, which had been arranged two years before, was celebrated, and a common policy was agreed between the two emperors. The conference was suddenly interrupted by the news that Maximin had crossed the Bosphorus.

Maximin had no doubt expected that his ally Maxentius would put up a stubborn resistance to Constantine's attack, and that Licinius would have been drawn into the struggle: his plan had been to attack Licinius in the rear while he was thus engaged. Constantine's lightning campaign and Maxentius' sudden collapse had thrown his plans out of joint, but he was convinced that he would be the next victim of Licinius and Constantine. He could gain nothing by delay: his only chance of survival was to strike first. The majority of Licinius' troops had been withdrawn to the Italian frontier: he had 70,000 men mobilized in Bithynia. Licinius was a parsimonious paymaster, whereas he was lavish with his soldiers. A quick victory might provoke a mass desertion of Licinius by his troops.

The garrison of Byzantium resisted Maximin's blandishments and assaults for eleven days. On their surrender Maximin marched on Heraclea, which delayed him a few more days, and then he advanced eighteen miles to the first post-station along the road leading westwards to Hadrianople. Here he was forced to halt, for during the few weeks that he had been held up at Byzantium and Heraclea, Licinius had been informed of his attack, and had raced from Milan to Hadrianople, picking up troops by the way, and now occupied the next post-station, eighteen miles ahead, with a force of 30,000 men.

On 30 April Maximin deployed his troops for battle. Licinius, despite the fact that he was outnumbered by more than two to one, accepted the challenge. For he did not rely on human resources alone. As his troops came into line they grounded their shields, removed their helmets, and, raising their arms to the sky, recited in unison, their officers dictating the words, the following prayer:

Highest God, we beseech thee, Holy God, we beseech thee; to thee we commend all justice, to thee we commend our safety, to thee we commend our empire. Through thee we live, through thee we are victorious and fortunate. Highest, Holy God, hear our prayers: we stretch out our arms to thee; hear us, Holy, Highest God.

The battle was swift and decisive. Maximin, flinging off his imperial robes and disguising himself as a slave, fled post-haste for the straits. He reached them in twenty-four hours, and in another twenty-four was back in Nicomedia. Then, having picked up his family and his ministers, he made for Cappadocia, where he resumed his imperial robes and collected troops for a second stand.

Licinius entered Nicomedia in triumph, and on 15 June issued the following constitution to the governor of Bithynia:

When both I, Constantine Augustus and also I, Licinius Augustus, had happily met at Milan, and debated all measures which pertained to the interest and security of the State, we considered that among other matters which we saw would benefit a large number of persons, the very first that required regulation was that wherein was comprised respect for the Divinity: that we should give both to the Christians and to all others free power of following whatever religion each individual wished, in order that whatever Divinity there be in the heavenly seat can be appeased and propitious to us and to all who are placed under our rule. Accordingly we considered that this policy was to be prudently and rightly adopted, so that we thought that no person should be denied the opportunity of devoting himself either to the cult of the Christians or to whatever religion he himself felt most suitable for himself: in order that the Highest Divinity, whose worship we practise with free hearts, can afford to us in all things his wonted favour and kindness. Accordingly your excellency must know that we have resolved that all kinds of conditions, which in previous communications addressed to your office appeared to apply to the case of the Christians, are to be removed, and that now everyone of those who have the same desire for observing the religion of the Christians is freely and unconditionally, without any interference or molestation, to hasten to observe it. We thought it proper to explain this very fully to your excellency, that you might know that we have given to the same Christians free and absolute liberty to practise their religion. While you see that we have granted this grace to them, your excellency will understand that others also have for the peace of our reign been similarly granted free and open liberty for their religion or cult, so that every individual may have free power to pursuing what worship he chooses. This we have resolved that we may not appear to diminish any worship or any religion. In the case of the Christians, we have decided to make the following additional regulations.

There follow orders for restoring forthwith to the community of the Christians their places of worship and their other property, whether they were still in the possession of the Treasury or had been sold or granted to private persons: the purchasers or grantees being promised ultimate compensation from the Treasury. 'So it will come about that, as has been explained above, the divine favour towards us, which we have experienced in such great events, will prosperously continue for all time, to our success and the public happiness.'

Maximin must have already felt some qualms about his

anti-Christian policy, for in the winter of 312-13 he had issued a constitution relaxing the persecution. This document opens with a curiously disingenuous historical preamble. Diocletian and Maximian, Maximin asserted, had very properly, seeing the worship of the gods neglected owing to the large numbers of persons who had adopted the Christian faith, endeavoured by disciplinary measures to recall the backsliders to the religion of the immortal gods. But he himself on his accession, in view of the large number of potentially useful citizens who were being driven from their homes by the authorities, had, he claimed, reversed this policy, and instructed his governors not to use violence, but to win over Christians by persuasion. Then Nicomedia, followed by other cities, had petitioned him to expel the Christians from their territories, and he had ultimately felt obliged to accede to their petitions. Nevertheless, he confirms his previous orders that no Christian is to suffer violence or molestation by the officials, but only to be encouraged by persuasion to return to the worship of the gods. Eusebius attributed this edict to pressure from Constantine and Licinius, but it was issued before they had met at Milan, and it was probably due to doubts that had arisen in Maximin's own mind. In 312 he had been defeated by the Christian king of Armenia, and in the following winter his dominions had been ravaged by famine and by an outburst of plague. Maximin may have felt that the God whom the Christians worshipped was a dangerous enemy.

His defeat by Licinius left no room for doubt, and he now hastily issued an edict granting full liberty of worship to the Christians and restoring to them their confiscated churches and property. But this belated repentance did not profit him. As Licinius advanced swiftly from Nicomedia, Maximin withdrew through the Cilician gates to Tarsus: at the gates he might hope to hold up Licinius long enough to mobilize his forces from the Oriental diocese. But Licinius' troops quickly forced the pass and Maximin committed suicide.

From these events it is possible to reconstruct what had passed at Milan. Constantine and Licinius had agreed on a common policy towards the Christians: the property of the Church was to be restored and full and untrammelled liberty of worship permitted. Licinius' edict bears signs, in its laborious insistence that both Christians and others were to enjoy toleration, of being a compromise, and there can be little doubt in which direction either emperor was pulling. Constantine had already in his own dominions gone further than mere restitution and toleration: it must then have been Licinius who insisted on a strict impartiality.

It would also appear that Constantine had urged Licinius, in his forthcoming campaign against Maximin, to place his armies under the protection of that Heavenly Power which had granted his own armies victory over Maxentius. This advice Licinius apparently accepted with reservation. He did not adopt the sign under which Constantine's men had fought, and he drafted a form of prayer which, while it should be acceptable to the Heavenly Power, could give no offence to any other god.

We possess two works written during these years by Christians, one in Latin in the dominions of Constantine, the other in Greek in those of Licinius. Lactantius, the author of the Latin treatise, *On the Deaths of the Persecutors*, had, after Maxentius' fall, returned to the West to be appointed tutor to Constantine's eldest son Crispus. The Greek work is the ninth book of the *Church History* of Eusebius, bishop of Caesarea. This great work had originally been planned in eight books to end with the recantation of Galerius in 311. When Maximin renewed the persecution, only to be defeated and perish after a vain recantation of his errors, Eusebius added another book to his history. He was later, after the persecution and fall of Licinius, to add a tenth book, and to revise what he had said about Licinius in the ninth, but the revision was so superficial that the original can easily be reconstructed.

In both these works Constantine and Licinius are jointly acclaimed as champions of Christianity against persecutors. Reading them, one would infer that Licinius was as much a Christian as Constantine. Lactantius asserts that the prayer with which Licinius opened battle against Maximin was dictated to him in a dream by an angel of God, just as he declares that Constantine was instructed in a dream to paint the mysterious monogram on his soldiers' shields before the battle of the Milvian Bridge. Eusebius speaks of 'the champions of peace and piety, Constantine and Licinius', and concludes his book with the triumphant sentence,

So when the impious had been purged away, the sovereignty that was theirs by right was preserved unshaken and ungrudged to Constantine and Licinius alone: they first of all purged away enmity to God from their lives, and, recognizing the blessings that God had bestowed upon them, demonstrated their love of virtue and of God, their piety and gratitude to the Divinity, by their legislation on behalf of the Christians.

In a sermon which he preached at Tyre he went yet further, declaring that

now, as never before in history, the emperors, who are above all men, acknowledging the honour they have received from him, spit in the faces of lifeless idols and trample underfoot the lawless laws of demons, laugh at the old traditional falsehoods, and acknowledge the One God alone as the benefactor of themselves and all men, and confess Christ as the Son of God and King of all.

The inference of the Christians that Licinius was a Christian was proved by subsequent events to be false. Can one say at this date that they were right in drawing the same conclusion about Constantine?

Constantine's pagan subjects have left little record of what they conceived his religious position to be, but some significant hints of their attitude have survived. The senate, in order to celebrate Constantine's victory, erected a triumphal arch. The arch still stands and its inscription runs :

To the Emperor Caesar Flavius Constantine, the Greatest, the Pious, the Fortunate, Augustus, because by the prompting of the Divinity and the greatness of his soul, he with his forces avenged the commonwealth with just arms both on the tyrant and on all his faction, the senate and people of Rome dedicated this triumphal arch.

We cannot tell who composed this inscription : it must have been approved by the Emperor, but it may well have been drafted by the senate. If so, the vague allusion to a nameless Divinity indicates that the senators believed that any mention of the immortal gods would be offensive to the Emperor. In other words, they must have believed him to be a Christian, for no other sect or creed was intolerant of the gods.

The same conclusion is to be drawn from the panegyric which a Gallic rhetorician addressed to him, when, after the conference of Milan, he had moved to Trèves to inspect the Rhine frontier. The speech is naturally devoted to Constantine's victory over Maxentius. The orator marvels at the Emperor's boldness in attacking, unsupported by his colleagues, the tyrant who had defied the armies of Severus and Galerius. He rebukes him for his rashness in having left three quarters of his troops to guard the Rhine frontier, and, ignoring the protests of his generals, in having attacked 100,000 men with a bare quarter of his forces. What, he asks, was the source of the Emperor's confidence? 'Surely,' he replies, 'you have some secret communion, Constantine, with that divine mind, which, delegating our care to lesser gods, deigns to reveal itself to you alone.' This passage is the only mention of gods in the plural in the whole speech, and even here they are carefully dissociated from the Emperor. The Divine Power which watches over Constantine is described in studiously vague terms; indeed, the peroration of the speech is a masterpiece of ambiguity:

Wherefore we pray thee, O highest creator of the world, whose names are as many as thou hast willed that there be tongues of men – for what thou thyself wishest to be called, we cannot know – whether there be in thee some divine power or intelligence, which being infused throughout the universe, thou art mingled in every element, and dost move of thine own self without the impulsion of any external force; or whether there be some power above every heaven, whereby thou lookest down upon thy handiwork from some higher peak of nature; to thee I say we pray, that thou mayest preserve this our Emperor for all ages.

The passage is eloquent of the embarrassment of the pagan orator, forced to avoid all mention of the immortal gods, but averse from sullying his lips with any allusion to the God of the Christians.

It would appear that Constantine was regarded as a Christian by both his Christian and his pagan subjects from the time that he entered Rome. And this conclusion was natural, since Constantine had not only granted liberty of worship to the Christians and restored their confiscated property to the churches, but had subsidized the clergy and granted them immunities, and had in so doing expressed his conviction that the proper conduct of the Christian cult was of vital import to the prosperity and security of the Empire. He had, moreover, painted on the shields of his soldiers a symbol which, though new and apparently of his own invention, could be interpreted as a monogram of Christ. And he had soon after his victory startlingly proclaimed his allegiance to the Cross. In a

public place in Rome he had caused to be erected a statue
of himself, holding in his right hand a cross, with this
inscription (if Eusebius has correctly translated it) below:
'By this sign of salvation, the true mark of valour, I saved
your city and freed it from the yoke of the tyrant, and
moreover having freed the senate and people of Rome,
restored them to their ancient honour and glory.'

Against all this evidence is to be set the imperial coinage. The types and legends of the coinage, which were frequently changed from year to year, were a recognized
vehicle of imperial propaganda. Nothing would have been
easier than to eliminate from them all allusion to the pagan
gods; for while it was common to place upon the coins
representations of the gods, there were many religiously
neutral types which were equally commonly used, celebrating the prosperity of the age, the valour of the armies,
the concord of the emperors, peace, victory or plenty. Even
if Constantine had hesitated to offend the great majority
of his subjects by placing distinctively Christian symbols
on his coins, he could, without exciting any adverse comment, have eliminated representations of the pagan gods.
Yet for the next five years the mints of Constantine's dominions continued to issue coins in honour of Hercules
the Victorious, Mars the Preserver, Jupiter the Preserver, and
above all the Unconquered Sun, the Companion of the
Augusti: the last-named continues to be honoured at one
mint down to 320. It is impossible to believe that these
issues can have been continued for so many years merely
by official inertia without exciting the notice of the Emperor. And at any rate one special issue must have received
his positive approval. This is a set of magnificent gold
medallions struck to celebrate the meeting of Constantine
and Licinius at Milan, showing the heads of Constantine
and the Sun side by side.

During the years that he authorized these pagan issues,

Constantine can hardly have been in the full sense of the word a Christian. He was undoubtedly a patron and a devotee of the Highest Divinity whom the Christians worshipped; but he does not yet seem to have realized that this divinity was a jealous God who tolerated no partners or even subordinates. The story of Constantine's conversion perhaps helps to explain his religious position in the years which followed.

Eusebius in his *Life of Constantine*, which he wrote soon after the Emperor's death in 337, is the first to record the heavenly vision of the Cross. He himself knew nothing of it when he wrote the ninth book of his *Church History* soon after the fall of Maxentius and Maximin. Lactantius, when he wrote his treatise *On the Deaths of the Persecutors* during the same period, knew nothing of it; according to him, it was in a dream on the night before the battle of the Milvian Bridge that Constantine was instructed to mark 'the heavenly sign of God' on the shields of the soldiers. This statement of Lactantius is evidence that Constantine's troops did bear the sacred monogram on their shields at the battle of the Milvian Bridge, but the dream may be no more historical than the angel who dictated to Licinius his monotheistic prayer.

But if the story of the heavenly vision is slow to make its appearance, it rests on the best of authority. For Eusebius informs us that 'the victorious Emperor himself told the story to me, the author of this work, many years afterwards, when I was esteemed worthy of his acquaintance and familiarity, and confirmed it upon oath'. The story that Constantine told Eusebius was this. While he was planning the campaign against Maxentius, he was worried as to how he could counteract the magical arts in which his rival was an adept, and he prayed unceasingly to the Divine Power which he and his father before him had worshipped. One afternoon, as he was marching somewhere with his army, he saw with his own eyes, as did all his army, a cross of light, superimposed upon the sun, and the words 'In this conquer' written in the sky. The following night Christ appeared to him in a vision with the sign that he had seen in the sky, and commanded him to make a copy of it to serve as his standard in war. Next day he summoned goldsmiths and workers in precious stones, and they, under his instructions, produced the famous Labarum. Eusebius describes this as he saw it, when in later years the Emperor allowed him to inspect it. It consisted of a tall pole and cross-bar plated with gold. Near the top of the pole was a wreath in gold and precious stones enclosing the ☧ monogram. From the cross-bar hung a gorgeously embroidered square banner, on which were portraits of the Emperor and the Caesars, his sons: the original Labarum would presumably have carried Constantine's image alone.

There is no reason to doubt the *bona fides* of either Eusebius or Constantine. The vagueness of the setting in which the incident is placed bears the stamp of truth. If the vision were a fiction it would surely have been placed at some dramatic moment, like Lactantius' dream, not when Constantine was marching 'somewhere' unspecified. It is indeed curious that there is no contemporary record of the heavenly vision, but it may well have been less conspicuous than Constantine imagined it later to have been. It is, moreover, evident from the way in which Eusebius introduces the story that Constantine had never given any publicity to his experience: it was only when they had got on to terms of intimacy that the Emperor revealed to him his proud secret.

What Constantine probably saw was a rare, but well-attested, form of the 'halo phenomenon'. This is a phenomenon analogous to the rainbow, and like it local and transient, caused by the fall, not of rain, but of ice crystals across the rays of the sun. It usually takes the form of mock suns or of rings of light surrounding the sun, but a cross of light with the sun in its centre has been on several occasions scientifically observed. The display may well have been brief and unspectacular, but to Constantine's overwrought imagination it was deeply significant. It was to the Sun that he now especially paid his devotion, and in his hour of need the Sun had sent him a sign; and that sign was the Cross, the symbol of the Christians. Whatever this signified, that Christ was a manifestation of the Unconquered Sun, or that the Sun was the symbol of the Heavenly Power whom the Christians worshipped, it was manifest that Christ, the Lord of the Cross, was to be his champion and protector.

It was not the Cross which Constantine used as the emblem of his new patron god, but a monogram, ☧, composed of the first two Greek letters of the word 'Christos', *chi* and *rho*. It was this sign that he painted on the shields of his soldiers before the final battle, and that he himself henceforth wore on his helmet: it was, moreover, the distinctive feature of the Labarum. From the careful description which Lactantius gives of its form, it is evident that the monogram was something new to him and his Latin public, and though it was commonly employed in Greek as an abbreviation for other words beginning with *chi* and *rho*, it appears never to have been used before Constantine's day as a Christian symbol. It must have been Constantine's own idea to make the abbreviation into a heraldic emblem of his divine champion.

Confident in the support of the Christian God, Constantine put his powers to a severe test. The Gallic orator who in the summer of 313 congratulated the Emperor on his victory of the previous autumn no doubt exaggerated the risks which he had run in order to magnify the glory of his final victory. But there was a considerable degree of truth in his remarks. Maxentius had very large forces at his disposal, and had taken great pains to ingratiate himself with his troops by lavish generosity. Not only Severus, but the great Galerius himself, had failed dismally in their efforts to unseat him. Yet Constantine embarked on his attack single-handed, and employed for it only a quarter of his troops. Such confidence is hardly explicable, had not Constantine felt himself assured of divine favour.

His spectacular victory naturally confirmed Constantine's faith in the Christian God, and he resolved to take appropriate measures to express his gratitude and to win further favour. He had apparently, even before his victory, attached to himself as his religious adviser a Spanish bishop, Hosius of Corduba, and he took his expert advice, as we have seen, in distributing benefactions to the Church. But there is no evidence that he sought or received instruction in the faith. He had not been converted by any human missionary, but by a heavenly sign from God himself, and he seems for the time being to have formed his own ideas on the appropriate way to win God's favour. This was in his view to grant liberty, subsidies and immunities to the body of initiates who conducted the cult of the Supreme Divinity, the Church. Soon he was to learn that discord in his Church was hateful to the Divinity, and that in order to maintain His favour he must preserve its unity and harmony. But he does not yet appear to have realized that he would offend the Supreme Divinity by paying respect to other gods, and in particular to the Unconquered Sun, whom he in some sort identified with the Christian God. Did not the Christians themselves meet for prayer on the day of the sun, and in their prayers turn towards the rising sun? And was it not written in their holy books that God was the Sun of Righteousness?

It may seem strange that the bishops, whom he met with increasing frequency, did not sooner enlighten him on this point. But they were probably only too thankful to secure toleration and favour after the horrors of persecution. Constantine, like Maximin, might change his mind: it was safer not to provoke the Emperor and meanwhile to receive the subsidies and immunities which he showered upon the Church. It would be a bold man who offered unsolicited advice to a Roman emperor, and none of the bishops seems to have felt called upon to instruct Constantine, much less to rebuke him for his errors.

Constantine's legislation during the next decade bears out this analysis of his religious position. On the one hand he extended additional privileges to the Church. In 318 he ordained that a civil suit might, with the consent of both parties, be removed to the jurisdiction of a bishop, even when it had already begun in an imperial court, and that the bishop's verdict should be final. In 321 he legalized bequests to the Church, and enacted that manumissions performed in church before the bishop should have full legal validity, the slaves so freed becoming Roman citizens, and furthermore that the clergy might free their own slaves by will with full legal effect. It was also probably during this period that Constantine built the Basilica Constantiniana in the Lateran, with its Baptistery, the Fons Constantini, and endowed them with lands bringing in an annual revenue of 4,390 and 10,234 *solidi* respectively. For the lands which were bestowed on these churches all lay in the West, mainly in Italy, Sicily and Africa, with small quantities in Gaul and Greece (which he acquired in 314), whereas other Roman churches, endowed later, were given eastern lands. Other laws show traces of Christian influence. In 316 he prohibited the branding of convicts on the face, 'that the face, which is formed in the likeness of the heavenly beauty, may not be disfigured', and in 320 he repealed the disabilities which Augustus had imposed on

celibates, male and female, and on married persons who
were childless.

His legislation on Sunday observance is a more doubtful
case. In March 321 he enacted that on 'the venerable day
of the Sun', the law-courts and all workshops should be
closed and the urban population should rest: the rural
population were, however, commanded to continue their
labours, lest by missing the right moment the crops provided by the Heavenly Providence should perish. A second
law, issued a few months later, confirms that 'the day
celebrated by the veneration of the Sun' ought not to be
occupied with contentious legal proceedings, but permits
manumissions and emancipations on Sundays. The idea of
Sunday as a day of rest is Christian, but it is noteworthy
that Constantine does not call it, according to the current
Christian practice, the Lord's Day, but on the contrary
emphasizes its sacredness to the Sun. It would appear that
Constantine imagined that Christian observance of the first
day of the planetary week was a tribute to the Unconquered Sun.

Various laws dealing with magic and divination also reveal the ambiguity of Constantine's position. The private
practice of both had long been illegal, and Constantine
was making no innovation in prohibiting them. Towards
magic he is, in a law dated 318, unusually mild, for while
he subjects to severe penalties those who employ magic
arts against the lives or the chastity of their neighbours, he
expressly permits spells for the cure of illness or for pre-
venting rain or hail storms from spoiling the vintage. He
deals with divination in three laws issued in 319 and 320.
In two of them he prohibits soothsayers from entering
private houses, even on the pretext of personal friendship
with the owner; the penalty is for the soothsayer to be
burned alive and for his host to be deported to an island

after confiscation of his property. In both laws persons wishing to foretell the future are expressly authorized to do so publicly in the temples – 'You who think it to your interest, go to the public altars and temples and celebrate the rites of your traditional faith; for we do not prohibit the ceremonies of past practice to be performed in the light of day.' The third law shows that Constantine did not, at this date, see any harm in consulting soothsayers himself on appropriate occasions. It runs:

If it be established that any part of our palace or of other public buildings has been struck by lightning, the practice currently observed should be maintained and the soothsayers be asked what it portends, and their reports having been carefully collected should be referred to our notice. Leave is also to be given to others for observing this custom, provided that they refrain from domestic sacrifices, which are specifically prohibited.

It has often been remarked that Constantine felt no scruple at retaining the title of Pontifex Maximus. This point is not very significant, since not only did Constantine himself continue to hold it in his later years, when he was undoubtedly a Christian, but later Christian emperors down to Gratian did the same. The title was a traditional appanage of the office of Augustus, and involved no participation in pagan rites. It merely gave its holder rights of supervision and control over religion, and was as such as useful to a Christian as to a pagan emperor. Nor is it significant that Constantine, in 312, authorized the creation of a new provincial priesthood of Africa in honour of his family, the *gens Flavia*. As will be explained later, the institutions devoted to the imperial cult were without difficulty secularized and continued to flourish under the Christian empire.

Constantine's conversion may be said to have been in a sense a religious experience, since, though his dominating motive was the achievement of worldly power, he relied for that end not on human but on divine aid. But it was not a spiritual experience. Constantine knew and cared nothing for the metaphysical and ethical teaching of Christianity when he became a devotee of the Christian God: he simply wished to enlist on his side a powerful divinity, who had, he believed, spontaneously offered him a sign. His conversion was initially due to a meteorological phenomenon which he happened to witness at a critical moment of his career. But this fortuitous event ultimately led to Constantine's genuinely adopting the Christian faith, to the conversion of the Roman Empire, and to the Christian civilization of Europe.

A Christian emperor had not reigned in Rome for six months before the great problem of the Christian state presented itself – the relations of the secular government to the ecclesiastical hierarchy and the degree to which that government is entitled or bound to exercise its authority in spiritual affairs. Constantine, it will be remembered, had, on the advice of Hosius, entrusted his benefactions to the African churches to Caecilian, bishop of Carthage, with instructions to distribute them to the clergy named in a schedule drawn up by Hosius. He had likewise instructed Anullinus, the proconsul of Africa, to grant immunity to the clergy 'in the Catholic Church over which Caecilian presides', and had ordered Anullinus and Patricius, the deputy-prefect of Africa, to repress certain persons whom he had learned were endeavouring 'to distract the people of the Holy and Catholic Church by some base pretence'.

On 15 April 313 Anullinus drafted the following despatch to the Emperor:

When I had received and adored the celestial letter of your majesty, my devotion caused it to be entered in my humility's files for Caecilian and those who serve under him and are called 'clerics', and urged them to unite by common consent, and since they appeared to be freed by the indulgence of your majesty from all sorts of public duties, to guard the sanctity of the Catholic law and serve the divine worship with due reverence. But after a few days certain persons appeared, with a crowd of people with them, who thought fit to speak against Caecilian, and offered to my devotion a sealed packet and an unsealed petition, and urgently requested that I should direct them to the sacred and venerable court of your godhead. My humility has caused them to be so directed, so that your majesty may decide the whole issue : Caecilian remains in his present status and their pleas have been entered. Enclosed are the two petitions, one sealed, headed 'Petition of the Catholic Church' (charges against Caecilian) handed in by the party of Majorinus, the other unsealed, attached to it.

The enclosed petition ran :

We pray you, most excellent Emperor Constantine, since you are of righteous stock, seeing that your father did not with the other emperors carry out the persecutions and Gaul is immune from this crime ; whereas there are disputes between us and the other bishops in Africa, we pray that your piety may order judges to be given to us from Gaul.

It is noteworthy that the dissident bishops do not appeal to Constantine as being a Christian himself : perhaps this startling fact had not yet won credence in Africa.

The origins of the controversy to which these documents allude go back to the days of the Great Persecution. When the imperial edict was promulgated, ordering the surrender of the scriptures and the dismantling of the churches, and prohibiting assemblies for Christian worship, the reaction of the bishops and clergy had been various. Many had tamely submitted, some had been openly defiant, others had pursued a middle course, either going into hiding or surrendering to the authorities heretical or secular books which they represented to be the holy scriptures. Feeling ran high between the rigorists, who denounced the evasions of the moderates, and the moderates, who in turn denounced the rigorists for courting martyrdom unnecessarily. Accusations of *traditio*, surrendering the scriptures, were freely bandied to and fro, for they were in the nature of things extremely difficult to disprove: any bishop not under arrest had a *prima facie* case against him. Mensurius, bishop of Carthage, the metropolitan see of all the African provinces, was a moderate. He had gone into hiding, taking with him the scriptures, but had left some heretical texts in his church for the authorities to seize. This action was disapproved by Secundus of Tigisis, the primate of Numidia, who claimed that when the local mayor and town council had sent two non-commissioned officers to demand the scriptures from him, he had boldly replied, 'I am a Christian and bishop, not a *traitor*,' and that when they had asked him to give them some literature, no matter what, that they could show to the authorities, he had still refused, on the analogy of Eleazar the Maccabee, who refused even to pretend to eat swine's flesh lest he should be a stumbling-block to others. A somewhat acrimonious correspondence ensued between Secundus and Mensurius, who went so far as to prohibit his congregation from paying honour to those who spontaneously informed the authorities that they were in possession of scriptures and refused to surrender them. He also spoke slightingly of large numbers of confessors who were 'criminals or debtors to the Treasury, who took advantage of the persecution, wishing to be rid of a life burdened by many debts, or thought they could thus purge and wash away their crimes – or at any rate make money and live like fighting cocks in prison on the charity of the Christians'.

Mensurius was subsequently summoned to Rome to answer for harbouring and refusing to surrender one of his deacons, Felix, who was charged with having published a seditious pamphlet against the Emperor. He was acquitted, but died on his return journey. When Maxentius restored liberty to the churches, the election of a successor was considered. An obvious candidate was the archdeacon, Caecilian, who was of the same school of thought as Mensurius; but he had many enemies, including a wealthy lady named Lucilla, whom he had rebuked for carrying about the bone of a martyr and kissing it before receiving communion. Moreover, the Numidian bishops, headed by Secundus, would not favour a faithful supporter of Mensurius. Caecilian appears to have taken time by the forelock, and before the Numidians could arrive, he was hastily elected by a few neighbouring bishops – three only, his opponents alleged, the minimum number for a valid election – acclaimed by the clergy and people, and consecrated by Felix, the bishop of the little town of Aptunga. Thus, when the more distant bishops arrived, they found themselves presented with a *fait accompli*. Indignant, they looked around for some flaw in the proceedings, and, as Caecilian's character was unassailable, they declared that Felix, his consecrator, was a *traditor*. Caecilian offered to be reconsecrated by them, but they naturally refused this compromise, and ignoring Caecilian's election as invalid, proceeded to elect one Majorinus, a protégé of Lucilla, to the throne of Carthage: Lucilla's money is alleged to have flowed freely during the council. Henceforth the Church in Africa was divided into two hostile camps – those who recognized Caecilian and those who recognized Majorinus. The former party was composed in the main of the moderates, and enjoyed the support of Rome and the Western Churches in general: the latter comprised the rigorists.

Constantine appears to have felt no qualms in accepting the appeal of the dissident African bishops. He naturally delegated the decision of the case to experts, but he did not exactly follow the suggestion of the petitioners. He selected three Gallic bishops, but to preside over them he appointed Miltiades, bishop of Rome, writing to him as follows:

Constantine Augustus to Miltiades, bishop of Rome, and to Marcus [the latter was elected pope more than twenty years later, and was perhaps at this time coadjutor of the aged Miltiades]. Whereas several dispatches have been sent to me by his excellency Anullinus, proconsul of Africa, in which it appears that Caecilian, the bishop of Carthage, is accused on many points by some of his colleagues in Africa; and it seems to me very serious that in those provinces, which the Divine Providence has spontaneously entrusted to my devotion, where there is a great multitude of people, the population should be found in a state of discord and continuing in that sad condition, and there should be differences between the bishops; I have decided that Caecilian himself, with ten bishops who appear to accuse him and ten others whom he himself considers necessary for his cause, should without delay sail to Rome, in order that he may there be heard, as you may find fitting to the most august law, before you and also Reticius and Maternus and Marinus, your colleagues, whom I have ordered to come to Rome with all speed for this purpose. In order that you may have the fullest knowledge on all these matters, I have enclosed in my letter copies of the documents dispatched to me by Anullinus, and have sent them to your previously mentioned colleagues. On receiving them your reverence will decide how the aforesaid case may be most carefully examined and justly determined, since it does not escape your diligence that I have such great respect for the lawful Catholic Church that I wish you to leave absolutely no division or discord anywhere. May the divinity of the Great God preserve you for many years, dearest sir.

Several points of interest emerge from this letter. Constantine had originally accepted Hosius' estimate of the African situation, that the opponents of Caecilian were wicked rebels. He is still convinced of the wickedness and danger of schism; that conviction was to remain deeply rooted in his mind to his dying day. But, having read the other side's case, he now takes up an independent and judicial attitude on the question of which party is guilty of the schism, and, deciding on his own authority that the issue is to be examined, he himself chooses the judges and summons the two parties. The letter to Miltiades has a curiously official tone; it reads like a minute to a civil servant.

Miltiades did not accept this position. The court, which met on 2 October in the palace of Fausta in the Lateran, consisted not only of the four bishops of Rome, Cologne, Autun and Arles whom Constantine had nominated, but of fifteen others from various Italian sees. The Pope had insisted that the proposed imperial commission of inquiry be transformed into a church council. Constantine henceforth accepted the custom of the Church that ecclesiastical issues should be decided by councils of bishops. He did not, however, abandon his prerogative of convening councils on his own initiative and summoning to them what bishops he chose; and he still reserved to himself, as the sequel will show, an appellate jurisdiction from church councils. In effect it was the Emperor who won the day, by converting the once independent councils of bishops into imperial commissions of inquiry.

By the time the council met Majorinus was dead. But the schism had been confirmed by the election by the dissidents of a new rival to Caecilian, Donatus, from whom the party were henceforth named the Donatists. The council gave judgement in favour of Caecilian, Miltiades summing up as follows:

Whereas it has been established that Caecilian is not accused by those who came with Donatus on the ground of his profession of faith and has not been convicted by Donatus on any point, I vote that he be deservedly maintained in his ecclesiastical communion with unimpaired status.

The Donatists refused to accept the verdict, on the ground that 'the whole case had not been heard, but rather the bishops had shut themselves up somewhere and passed judgement as convenient for themselves'. Constantine, though with an ill grace, allowed the appeal, and summoned a larger council to meet at Arles on 1 August in the following year, 314. His sentiments are revealed by two documents: his letter of summons addressed to Chrestus, bishop of Syracuse, and the letter which he wrote to the deputy praetorian prefect of Africa, instructing him to dispatch Caecilian with a number of his supporters and opponents to Arles.

In the preamble of both letters he recapitulates the steps that he had previously taken to decide the controversy; in the second he strongly emphasizes his own initiative in the matter, and speaks of the council of Rome as a body of imperial commissioners, 'who reported to me in their official record all the proceedings which had taken place before them, and who verbally assured me that this verdict was based on the equity of the case'. In both letters he comments adversely on the attitude of the Donatists, who, 'forgetting their own salvation and the reverence which they owe to the most holy sect, and still even now persisting in their private enmities', had refused to accept the judgement of the Roman council. 'The result', he adds, 'is that these very persons who ought to practise brotherly and harmonious concord shamefully and indeed sinfully quarrel with one another, and afford an occasion for mockery to men whose souls are alienated from this most holy worship.'

Constantine's anxiety for the reputation of the Church among the pagans is interesting. Still more interesting is the fear which he expresses in a postscript to his official:

Since I am informed that you too are a worshipper of the Highest God, I will confess to your gravity that I consider it absolutely contrary to the divine law that we should overlook such quarrels and contentions, whereby the Highest Divinity may perhaps be moved to wrath, not only against the human race, but also against me myself, to whose care He has, by His celestial will, committed the government of all earthly things, and that He may be so far removed as to take some untoward step. For I shall really and fully be able to feel secure and always to hope for prosperity and happiness from the ready kindness of the most mighty God, only when I see all venerating the most holy God in the proper cult of the catholic religion with harmonious brotherhood of worship.

This passage is the key to Constantine's whole religious position. He believed that the Highest Divinity, whom the Christian Church worshipped, had given him victory and dominion; he hoped by doing His will to win by His favour further prosperity for himself and his subjects, and he feared of offending Him to be cast down from power and to involve the empire in his ruin.

The first and most obvious measure to win the favour of the Supreme Divinity was to give His Church liberty, wealth and immunity to carry on His worship without distraction. The results of the opposite policy were triumphantly pointed out by the Christian writers of this period, whose constant theme is the doom which had overtaken the persecuting emperors one by one; Lactantius wrote a whole treatise *On the Deaths of the Persecutors*, and Eusebius emphasized the same moral in each succeeding edition of his *Church History*. But now Constantine was learning that favours to the Church were not enough. The Supreme Divinity demanded unity in His Church, and was bitterly offended by schism among His worshippers. Therefore it was Constantine's duty as emperor, in order to keep his favour for the Empire, to impose unity on the Church.

Thirty-three bishops duly met at Arles on 1 August 314, and confirmed the verdict of the council of Rome, ruling further

concerning those who are said to have betrayed the holy scriptures or the sacred vessels or the names of their brothers, that whoever of them is convicted from the public records, not by bare words, shall be removed from the ranks of the clergy ... And since there are many who seem to fight against the law of the Church and think that they ought to be admitted to accuse by means of hired witnesses, let them not be admitted at all, unless, as we stated above, they prove their case by the public records.

They also took the opportunity of passing a number of canons, or resolutions on Church discipline, ordering for instance that Easter be kept everywhere on the same day, to be notified annually by the bishop of Rome; that priests should stay in the city in which they were ordained, and that the clergy should not practise usury. Charioteers and actors were excommunicated so long as they followed their professions. On the other hand, Christian soldiers were excommunicated if 'they threw away their arms in peace'. This brief phrase is obscure, but is apparently directed against conscientious objectors, such as the centurion Marcellus, who had torn off his uniform and refused to serve any longer, while excusing those who threw away their arms in the stress of battle. Another canon gives a rather grudging assent to Christians holding provincial governorships or other public offices. They are to be given letters of recommendation to the bishops of the area in which they are to serve, and are only to be excommunicated if in their judgement they misbehave.

At the same time that he was summoning the council of Arles, Constantine set on foot an independent judicial investigation on what was, legally, the key-point of the controversy: whether Felix, the bishop of Aptunga, who had consecrated Caecilian, was or was not a *traditor*. We possess, in a somewhat mutilated and corrupt manuscript, the official verbatim record of these proceedings. It is a fascinating document, most revealing of the hectoring and sometimes brutal methods of the Roman courts, but it is unfortunately far too long to give in full. The case turned on the evidence of Alfius Caecilianus, who had, in the year of the Great Persecution, now eleven years ago, been one of

the two annual magistrates (*duoviri*) of Aptunga. He was
summoned by Aelius Paulinus, the deputy-prefect of Africa, to attend at Carthage on 19 August 314 together with
the clerk and the recorder whom he had employed during
his year of office, and the official records of his proceedings.
The recorder was dead, and the official records could not
be found: Caecilianus had apparently taken them to his
own home on his retirement and lost them. But Caecilianus and Miccius, his clerk, duly appeared.

Before the city council of Carthage, Alfius Caecilianus
deposed as follows:

I had gone to Zama to buy linen yarn with Saturninus, and
when we returned to town, the Christians themselves sent to
me at the town hall and said: 'Has the imperial order reached
you?' I said, 'No; but I have seen copies already, and at Zama
and Furni I saw the churches being pulled down and the scriptures being burned. So bring out any scriptures you have in
obedience to the imperial command.' Then they sent to the
house of Felix the bishop to take out the scriptures from there,
so that they could be burnt according to the imperial order. So
Galatius went with me to the place where they used to hold their
prayer meetings. We took out the throne and the letters of
greeting, and all the doors were burnt according to the imperial
order. And when we sent to the house of the same Felix the
bishop, the town officials reported that he was away.

So far Felix seemed to be cleared, but Maximus, counsel
for the Donatist party, produced a letter from Caecilianus
to Felix which ended:

You said, 'Take away the key, and the rolls you will find on
the throne and the books on the stone. Take them. Of course,
see that your officials do not take the oil and wheat.' And I
said to you, 'Don't you know that the actual building in which
the scriptures are found must be demolished?' And you said:
'What are we to do then?' And I said to you: 'Get one of your
men to take them into the yard, where you hold your prayers,

and let them be put there. And I will come with my officials and remove them.' And we came there and removed them all according to the imperial order.

This letter was alleged to have been written at the dictation of Caecilianus by a scribe named Ingentius. Caecilianus admitted the letter to be his, but denied that he had dictated the passage quoted.

A further session was held on 15 February next year before Aelianus, proconsul of Africa, acting on behalf of Verus, Aelius Paulinus' successor as deputy-prefect, who was ill. Ingentius was produced, and by dint of vigorous prompting by Apronianus, counsel for the Catholic party, and by the proconsul himself, together with the threat of torture, which was eventually not applied when Ingentius claimed to be a town councillor, was induced to make the following confession, which Caecilianus confirmed. Wishing to spite Felix for having denounced a Donatist friend as a *traditor*, he had come to Caecilianus, pretending that Felix had sent him to ask Caecilianus to help him out of a difficulty: Felix had disposed of some valuable copies of the scriptures entrusted to his care, and their return was now demanded; would Caecilianus mind writing him a letter declaring that they had been seized and burnt in the persecution? Caecilianus had indignantly refused to be party to this dishonest trick: 'Is this the honour of the Christians?' he had exclaimed, and had dictated a letter to Felix, giving a true account of his proceedings during the persecution. Undeterred by the failure of his trick, Ingentius had taken this letter, added the incriminating sentences, and produced it as evidence against Felix.

On the basis of this evidence the proconsul Aelianus declared Felix innocent of the charge of having surrendered or burned the scriptures, and committed Ingentius to prison for more rigorous examination. Constantine, on being informed of these results, wrote to Probianus, Aelianus' successor, ordering Ingentius to be sent under escort to his court,

in order that those who are in my presence and never cease appealing, day in day out, may hear and be actually present while it is proved and demonstrated that it is futile for them to wish to create prejudice against the bishop Caecilian and rise violently against him. For so it will result that such quarrels will be abandoned, as they should be, and the people will without any dissension serve their own religion with due reverence.

For the Donatist party, with invincible faith in the rightness of its cause, had refused to accept the judgement of the council of Arles, and had appealed again, this time to the Emperor himself. Constantine's letter to the assembled bishops on receiving this news is a most interesting document, revealing how he was progressing in the faith. It begins on a personal note.

The eternal and religious piety of our God, which passes all understanding, does not allow our human condition to wander long in darkness, nor suffers the hateful wishes of some to prevail so far that He does not by His own most glorious light once again open the path of salvation and grant that they be turned to the rule of righteousness. I know this by many examples. I draw this same conclusion from my own case. For originally there were in me many things which seemed to lack righteousness. And I did not think that a power above could see any thoughts which I harboured in the secret places of my heart. What fortune did these thoughts, being such as I have said, deserve to receive? Surely one abounding with every evil. But Almighty God, sitting on high, has granted what I did not deserve; certainly now the blessings which he has granted in his heavenly kindness to me his servant cannot be told or counted, most holy bishops of Christ the Saviour, dearest brothers.

He goes on to express his joy that some of the Donatists have, by the grace of God, been recalled to the light by the council, and his horror at the obstinacy of the remainder.

They demand my judgement, who am myself waiting for the judgement of Christ. For I say – and it is the truth – that the judgement of priests ought to be regarded as if the Lord Himself sat in judgement.... They seek the things of the world, abandoning heavenly things. What frenzied audacity! As is done in the eyes of the pagans, they have interposed an appeal. The pagans sometimes, to avoid the lower courts where justice can be quickly obtained, prefer to have recourse to the authority of a higher court by interposing an appeal. What shall I say of these detractors of the law, who, rejecting the judgement of heaven, have thought fit to demand mine?

Constantine finally orders the bishops to return to their sees, informing them that he has given instructions for the recalcitrant Donatist bishops to be sent to his court, 'there to live, there to see before them something worse than death', and has also ordered the deputy-prefect of Africa to send forthwith to his court any who there support their cause, 'lest in the future, under the great glory of our God, things may be done by them which may excite the greatest anger of the heavenly providence'.

It is evident that at this stage Constantine had no intention of allowing the appeal of the Donatists. He was soon after called away by a war, which will be recounted in the next chapter, not returning to Rome till 21 July 315. By this time his temper had cooled, and he granted the imprisoned Donatist bishops permission to return to Africa and promised them a hearing of the case.

Soon afterwards he changed his mind. 'Since I know,' he wrote to the Donatist bishops,

that some of your party are somewhat turbulent and obstinately pay little regard to a right verdict and the simple truth, and that it may perhaps come about that if the case is tried on the spot, the affair will not be terminated as it should and as the truth demands, and through your excessive obstinacy something may occur which could both displease the Heavenly Divinity and reflect greatly on my reputation, which I always wish to remain unsullied, I have decided, as I said, that Caecilian should rather, as previously arranged, come here; and I believe that he will, in deference to my letter, shortly arrive. I promise you that if in his presence you can by yourselves prove anything on one single charge or crime, I shall regard this as if every accusation which you bring against him has been proved. May Almighty God grant peace everlasting.

It must have been about this time that Constantine ordered that Ingentius the forger should be brought to Rome, and it was no doubt in his jubilation at having obtained legal proof of the validity of Caecilian's orders that he made this bold challenge.

What happened next is rather obscure. Caecilian, for reasons unknown, failed to attend at the date fixed at Rome and the Donatists, claiming that the case had gone by default against him, endeavoured to leave the city. Constantine had them arrested and brought to Milan, whither he had moved. When Caecilian eventually arrived, the Emperor apparently did not try the case, but decided to attempt a compromise. Caecilian was interned at Brescia, and meanwhile two bishops, Eunomius and Olympius, were sent to Carthage to consecrate a third bishop to supersede the two disputants. Their proceedings provoked rioting by the Donatist party, and after six weeks they abandoned their mission, declaring for the legitimacy of Caecilian's clergy. Donatus next escaped and returned to Carthage and Caecilian followed him. Constantine now released the rest of the imprisoned Donatist clergy, by now reduced to four bishops and one priest, who had been dragged in his train to Trèves; their travel warrant, dated 26 February, authorizing their conveyance by the public post to Arles and thence by sea to Africa, with board during the journey, has been by a curious chance preserved. The Emperor instructed Domitius Celsus, the deputy-prefect of Africa, to investigate the riots which had occurred, and his action provoked further rioting. The victims of the government's repressive measures were acclaimed by the Donatists as martyrs.

The situation was getting out of hand, and that largely by Constantine's own fault. By his hesitant policy he had encouraged the hopes of the Donatists. Constantine now resolved to face the issue squarely, and he wrote again to Domitius Celsus, ordering him to suspend proceedings against the Donatists, and at the same time announce to both parties

that with the favour of the divine piety I shall come to Africa and shall most fully demonstrate, by pronouncing a clear judgement, to all, both Caecilian and those who appear to oppose him, what kind of veneration is to be rendered to the Highest Divinity and what sort of worship appears to please Him. . . . And since it is obvious enough that no one can gain the blessings of a martyr from that crew who seem to be alienated and divorced from the truth of religion, I shall without any hesitation cause those whom I shall judge hostile to the divine law and to religion itself, and shall find guilty of violence against the proper worship, to pay the penalty which their mad and reckless obstinacy deserves.

Constantine was moving fast to Caesaropapism. 'I,' he concludes,

am going to make plain to them what kind of worship is to be offered to the Divinity. For in no other way do I believe that I can escape the greatest guilt, than by refusing to connive at this wickedness. What higher duty have I in virtue of my imperial office and policy than to dissipate errors and repress rash indiscretions, and so to cause all to offer to Almighty God true religion, honest concord and due worship?

This fiery pronouncement ended, like so many of Constantine's valiant words, in smoke. Constantine postponed his visit to Africa, and eventually abandoned it. In the autumn of 316 he gave judgement on Caecilian's case at Milan, setting forth the full story of the successive episcopal decisions, and ending:

I have seen that Caecilian is a man endowed with all innocence, performing the proper functions of his religion, and serving it as was his duty, and it has clearly appeared that no crime can be found in him, such as had been concocted against him in his absence by the deceit of his enemies.

This judgement was notified to Eumalius, the deputy-prefect of Africa, in a letter dated 10 November 316, but no punitive measures such as Constantine threatened were taken against the Donatists.

Four years later Silvanus, the Donatist bishop of Cirta, one of those who had ordained Majorinus, the first schismatic bishop of Carthage, quarrelled with one of his deacons, Nundinarius. Nundinarius in revenge charged him with having, in the year of the persecution, when a subdeacon of the church of Cirta, been a *traditor*, and produced a great deal of evidence discreditable to the leading Donatist bishops. The case was tried before Zenophilus, consular of Numidia, on 13 December 320, and again we possess the official verbatim record of a large part of the proceedings.

The most startling document produced was the alleged minutes of an episcopal council, held at Cirta on 4 or 5 March, or May, 304 or 305 (the dating of various copies differed), attended by a number of Numidian bishops later prominent in the Donatist party. The text runs:

When Secundus, bishop of Tigisis, the primate, had taken the chair in the house of Urbanus Donatus, he said: 'Let us first test ourselves and so we shall be able to ordain a bishop here.'
Secundus [to Donatus of Mascula]: 'It is said that you were a *traditor*.'
Donatus: 'You know how Florus sought to make me sacrifice, but God did not deliver me into his hands, brother: since God has acquitted me, do you preserve me for God.'

Secundus: 'What are we going to do about the martyrs, then? It was because they were not *traditores* that they were crowned.'

Donatus: 'Send me to God: there I will make my reckoning.'

Secundus: 'Stand on one side.'

Secundus [*to Marinus of Aquae Tibilitanae*]: 'It is said that you were a *traditor* too.'

Marinus: 'I gave Pollus some papers, for my books are safe.'

Secundus: 'Go to one side.'

Secundus [*to Donatus of Calamae*]: 'It is said that you were a *traditor*.'

Donatus: 'I gave up some medical books.'

Secundus: 'Go to one side.'

Secundus [*to Victor of Rusicada*]: 'It is said that you handed over four gospels.'

Victor: 'Valentianus was mayor: he himself forced me to deliver them to the flames. I knew they were defective copies: forgive me this fault, and God also will forgive me.'

Secundus: 'Stand on one side.'

Secundus [*to Purpurius of Limiata*]: 'It is said that you killed the two sons of your sister.'

Purpurius: 'Do you think you can bully me like the rest? What did you do when *you* were arrested by the mayor and council to make you surrender the scriptures? How did *you* free yourself from them, unless by surrendering something or ordering it to be surrendered? They did not let you out for nothing. Yes, I did kill, and I do kill those who attack me; so don't provoke me to say more; you know that I do not care for anyone's feelings.'

Secundus junior [*to his uncle Secundus*]: 'You hear what he says against you. He is prepared to secede and make a schism, not he only, but all whom you are accusing. I know that they can depose you and pass sentence on you, and you will be left the only heretic. So what does it matter to you what they each did? They can make their reckoning with God.'

Secundus [*to three other bishops*]: 'What is your opinion?'

They replied: 'They have God with whom they can make their reckoning.'

Secundus: 'You and God know : take your seat.'
All replied : 'Thanks be to God.'

The reader may judge for himself whether the minutes of so incriminating a meeting are likely to have been taken or preserved. But whether the evidence was true or false, it was accepted by the court; and now that the Donatist leaders had been exposed as being guilty of the very sin that they alleged against their opponents, Constantine was emboldened to take coercive measures against the party. Their leaders were banished, they were deprived of the churches which they held, and any building which they used as a place of worship was ordered to be confiscated. The first persecution of Christians by a Christian government began.

Persecution only hardened the fanatical temper of the Donatists. To the Emperor's last appeal for unity, they sent the defiant reply that 'never would they communicate with his scoundrelly bishop, and that they were prepared to suffer whatever he chose to inflict upon them'. And they were as good as their word : rather than submit to the authority of the *traditores*, they endured imprisonment, torture and even death.

Constantine soon sickened of the rôle of persecutor. On 5 May 321, when his coercive policy had been in force for only three months, he sent a dispatch to Verinus, deputy-prefect of Africa, in which, after severely denouncing the Donatists as enemies of Christian peace, he ordered that their exiles should be restored and toleration should be extended to them; he left them to the judgement of God, who had already begun to take vengeance upon them. At the same time, in a letter to the Catholic bishops of Africa he explained his policy. All his efforts to establish concord had been frustrated by the obstinate wickedness of a few : he had exhausted every human means, and now he could only leave the remedy to God. Meanwhile, he urged them to cultivate patience, and to endure quietly whatever injuries their opponents might inflict upon them. Let there be no retaliation, for vengeance was of God. The patient endurance of the malice of the Donatists would rank in his eyes as martyrdom.

This letter suggests that the Donatists did not confine themselves to passive resistance. The Donatist controversy was probably already developing into the species of class war which it later became. From the beginning there had no doubt been a class bias in the controversy. The upper classes had lapsed in large numbers during the persecutions or practised evasion, and they naturally favoured bishops like Mensurius, who justified evasion and deprecated fanaticism. The confessors and martyrs, on the other hand, were mainly drawn from the lower classes, and the masses tended to rally to those bishops who gave them high honour and unsparingly denounced those who weakened or lapsed. As the conflict developed, the wealthy tended more and more to rally to the Catholics, as the governmental party, and the poor supported the Donatists, just because they were rebels against the established order. Soon Donatist outlaws were making it unsafe for Catholic moneylenders to collect their interest from the peasants, and Catholic landlords, travelling to their estates, were being compelled to dismount and run before their own carriages, while their slaves drove.

In his first attempt to establish concord in the Church, Constantine had been obliged to admit defeat: he had handed back to the Supreme Divinity the task which he had charged him to perform. It was beyond his powers, as it was to prove beyond the powers of all his successors. The Donatist schism outlasted the Vandal conquest of Africa, the reconquest by Justinian, and the final overthrow of Christian rule by the Arabs. Only when Christianity perished did the schism cease.

But in the course of the struggle Constantine unawares achieved a victory over the Church. He claimed, and the Church admitted, his right as emperor to adjudicate ecclesiastical disputes, whether through councils of bishops, summoned at his behest, or in his own person. He claimed – and once again the Church raised no protest – to exile bishops, seize churches and prohibit religious meetings. The Church had acquired a protector, but it had also acquired a master.

8 The Crusade against Licinius

Despite his marriage with Constantia and the agreement reached on religious policy at Milan, Licinius must have viewed Constantine from the first with resentment and suspicion. It cannot have pleased him that Constantine should have arrogated to himself the position of senior Augustus, and he may well have doubted whether his young and energetic colleague's ambition would long be limited to the West. Constantine seems, if that story told by later chroniclers is true, to have done his best to allay these fears; for in 314, despite the fact that Licinius now, by his conquest of Maximin's dominions, controlled the larger and richer half of the Empire, he suggested handing over Italy to a new Caesar, a certain Bassianus, to whom he had married another of his half-sisters, Anastasia. This suggestion led to a quarrel between the two Augusti. Bassianus' brother, Senecio, was in the service of Licinius, and through him Licinius attempted to seduce Bassianus from his loyalty to Constantine. Constantine arrested and executed Bassianus and demanded the surrender of Senecio, which Licinius refused. Both sides then prepared for war. Constantine issued a series of coins, on which he advertised the legitimacy of his position, honouring his putative imperial ancestor Claudius Gothicus, his father Constantius, and – brazenly ignoring the manner of his death – Maximian, who had first granted him the title of Augustus. Licinius overthrew Constantine's statues at the frontier city of Emona in Pannonia.

Immediately after the conference of Milan, Constantine had crossed the Alps to deal with a threatened invasion of Gaul by the Franks. No sooner had he reached the Lower German province where the attack was expected, than he was recalled southwards by trouble on the Upper Rhine. The Franks were encouraged by the Emperor's departure to launch their attack, but Constantine surprised them by shipping his army down the river and inflicted on them a resounding defeat. He remained at Trèves for the next twelve months, then in the late summer of 314 marched eastwards with 20,000 men to invade Licinius' dominions. The first battle was fought at Cibalae, between the Sava and the Drava, on 8 October, and Licinius, despite his superiority in numbers – he is stated to have had 35,000 men under his command – was defeated with heavy loss. He hastily retreated to Sirmium, removed thence his wife and son and his treasury, and marched down the Danube into Dacia; Constantine, following up his victory, occupied Sirmium.

Licinius now proclaimed Valens, the general in charge of the Lower Danube garrison, as Caesar, presumably in order to ensure his loyalty, concentrated his forces at Hadrianople, in Thrace, and, having thus recovered himself, proposed peace to Constantine. The delegates of the two Emperors met at Philippi, but failed to agree, and the war was renewed. A second battle was fought on the plain of the Arda: it was stubbornly contested and indecisive, and in the following night the two armies missed one another, Constantine pressing on to Byzantium, whither he thought Licinius would retreat, and Licinius withdrawing northwest to Beroe. Having thus cut each other's communications, the two Emperors entered on a second parley, and this time came to terms.

Constantine was to annex the two dioceses of Pannonia and Moesia, leaving to Licinius only Thrace out of his previous European dominions. Valens was deposed and executed, and it appears to have been proposed that Constantine's eldest son (by Minervina), Crispus, and the newly born Constantine, Fausta's first boy, together with Licinius' son, Licinius, should be proclaimed Caesars. Licinius actually issued some coins in honour of the three new Caesars, but for reasons unknown the project was abandoned for the time being – it was not till 1 March 317 that Crispus, Constantine junior and Licinius junior were inaugurated as Caesars.

Constantine and Licinius celebrated their reconciliation by sharing the consulate for the year 315, and during the next five or six years their amity remained apparently unbroken. Constantine spent the first six months of 315 inspecting his new dominions, and then, after a short visit to Rome, returned to Gaul. In the autumn of 316 he moved again to the Balkans, and there he remained for the next eight years, save for a visit to Milan in the summer of 318. He seems during this period to have left Gaul in the nominal charge of the Caesar Crispus (who cannot have been much over twelve when he was proclaimed in 317). In 320 Crispus won his spurs in a campaign against the Alamans on the Upper Rhine, and in the following year a Gallic orator speaks of him as spending the years of his boyhood in military triumphs.

The first sign of discord appeared in 321, when Constantine proclaimed his two sons, Crispus and Constantine, consuls without Licinius' consent. In 322 he again nominated consuls of his own choice without obtaining his colleague's agreement. In this year Constantine crossed the Danube and conducted a successful campaign against the Sarmatians. In 323 once again Constantine's consuls were not acknowledged in the East. This spring Constantine undertook a campaign against the Goths, who had overrun and pillaged both his diocese of Moesia and Licinius' diocese of Thrace. In the course of this campaign Constantine trespassed on his neighbour's dominions: Licinius protested, Constantine refused satisfaction, and next spring war began.

While it is clear, on the evidence available, that Constantine was the aggressor in his final struggle with Licinius, it does not follow that his unprovoked attack was due merely to ambition. During the years that preceded the rupture, the two men had been steadily drifting apart in their religious views and policy. Licinius had at first loyally observed the agreement reached at Milan, but, it would seem, somewhat against the grain. He had probably never been convinced that the Holy, Highest God, whom he had invoked with such success against Maximin, was the curious divinity whom the Christians worshipped, and he tended more and more to identify him with Jupiter Optimus Maximus, the Preserver, the only god who figures on his coinage after 313. On the numismatic evidence, Licinius appears to have been a more convinced monotheist than Constantine was at this date; but Licinius did not deny the other gods, whom he doubtless regarded as variant aspects or emanations of Jupiter.

As Constantine's favour to the Christians became more pronounced, Licinius began to view them with growing hostility, suspecting – rightly enough – that their prayers were for his rival rather than for himself. Eventually he began a series of vexatious measures against the Church. Councils were prohibited, and bishops were even forbidden to visit one another's cities. This was a shrewd blow, for not only were councils essential for settling disputes which might arise on doctrine or discipline, but no bishops could be consecrated save by a meeting of other bishops. Next, in the interests of morality, he forbade men and women to worship together, and prohibited bishops from instructing women, ordering them to appoint female teachers. And in the interests of public health, he ordered that meetings for worship should not be held in churches within the city walls, but in the open outside the gates. At the same time he purged first his court, and later the whole civil service, of Christians, by imposing pagan sacrifice as a test for office. The execution of all these decrees naturally provoked resistance, and a number of bishops were arrested and some executed, while in some cities churches were demolished.

This rather half-hearted persecution gave Constantine a justification for what had no doubt been a long-cherished ambition. Surely he owed it to the Supreme Divinity who had entrusted him with authority over half the Roman world to overthrow the tyrant who oppressed His worshippers in the other half. Such a war would be no ordinary civil war like that against Maxentius: that campaign had been fought under the auspices of the Christian God, but hardly for His sake; for Maxentius had been tolerant and even friendly to the Christians. The forthcoming campaign would be a veritable crusade, and Constantine resolved to make it so. From the year 320 onwards the last survivor of the pagan gods, the Unconquered Sun, finally vanishes from his coinage.

The Emperor summoned Christian bishops to assist him in his preparations. A special tent was equipped as a portable private chapel for the Emperor when on campaign: we are told by Eusebius that in the subsequent war Constantine would at critical moments retire to it for prayer, to emerge inspired with the next tactical move. The sacred standard, the Labarum, was provided with a special guard of fifty men, picked not only for their strength and courage but for their piety, whose sole duty it would be to carry it to wherever danger threatened on the battlefield. It was probably at this time that Constantine set on foot the Christian propaganda in the army which Eusebius

later describes. Christian soldiers were given leave on
Sundays to enable them to attend divine worship, and the
pagan majority were marched off to a compulsory parade;
where they were made to recite a prayer which should be
acceptable to the Highest Divinity :

Thee alone we know to be God. Thee do we confess to be
King. Upon Thee do we call for aid, from Thee have we gained
our victories, through Thee have we prevailed over the enemy.
Thee we thank for past and from Thee we hope future benefits,
Thee do we all beseech, begging Thee long to preserve for us our
emperor Constantine and his God-loving sons safe and victorious.

Licinius took up the challenge on behalf of the old gods.
He summoned to his side priests and soothsayers and magi-
cians from Egypt, placated the gods with sacrifice and
asked their will through Oracles. Eusebius records a speech
delivered by him to his council shortly before the opening
of the war, which is probably in substance genuine; for he
assures us that members of the audience reported it to him
shortly afterwards. He and his party, he declared, were
worshippers of the ancestral gods, his opponent was an
atheist, who erroneously worshipped some strange god,
and disgraced his army with his shameful emblem. The
result of the coming war would prove whether the old
gods were the true saviours, or Constantine's god, wherever
he hailed from. If he were defeated, he would, he ironic-
ally admitted, have no alternative but to abandon the old
gods and worship their new-fangled conqueror. But if he
won – and he would win – he would follow up his victory
by war against the atheists.

In the spring of 324 Constantine heralded his forthcoming attack by once again parading on his coins his imperial
ancestors, Claudius Gothicus and Constantius, together
with Maximian. Both sides had mustered far larger forces
than had been employed in the previous wars of the century.

Licinius had marshalled 150,000 infantry and 15,000 cavalry, drawn from the famous horsebreeding areas of Phrygia and Cappadocia. He had also collected a fleet of 350 ships from his maritime provinces, Libya and Egypt, Phoenicia and Cyprus, Caria, Asia and Bithynia. Constantine's land forces, 120,000 of all arms, were almost as numerous as his rival's and of better quality, being drawn from the warlike provinces of Gaul and Illyricum, and seasoned in many frontier wars against the Franks, Alamans, Sarmatians and Goths. His fleet was very inferior, comprising only 200 thirty-oared galleys; he had also collected 2,000 merchantmen to transport his army across the straits and bring forward supplies. He himself commanded the army: the fleet he entrusted to the young Caesar, Crispus.

Constantine took the initiative, advancing from Thessalonica into Thrace, where Licinius awaited him in a very strong position at Hadrianople. Here, on 3 July, was fought the first battle of the war. There was a prolonged struggle, in which Constantine personally played a prominent part, being wounded in the thigh, and the Labarum proved its value, heartening his men whenever they were hard-pressed. Eusebius subsequently heard from the Emperor's own lips wonderful tales of its magical virtue, how it intercepted all missiles hurled at its bearer, but when one of the men deputed to carry it had shirked his duty and handed it on to his neighbour, he was promptly shot through the stomach. Eventually the discipline of Constantine's men prevailed over Licinius' superior numbers and strong defensive position, and Licinius was obliged to retreat with heavy loss to Byzantium.

Here he proclaimed his Master of the Offices, Martinianus, joint Augustus with himself. He was confident that with his command of the sea he could hold Byzantium as his European bridgehead indefinitely, until he could muster reinforcements from Asia and take the offensive. Constantine pressed the siege vigorously, building mounds against the walls and surmounting them with towers, from which his engines commanded the town. But with supplies and reinforcements flowing freely in by sea to his enemy, he made little progress, and he resolved to challenge Licinius by sea. Crispus was ordered to force the Hellespont.

Abantus, Licinius's admiral, had shown singularly little initiative. Despite his greatly superior strength, he made no attempt to attack Crispus in the Aegean, but allowed himself to be bottled up in the Hellespont, where his numbers were of relatively little use to him, Crispus worked his way up to Callipolis, and here, making skilful use of wind and currents, inflicted a crushing defeat upon him, sinking 130 ships, Licinius realized that his position was untenable, and crossed the Bosphorus to Chrysopolis. Constantine quickly reduced Byzantium, and ferried his men across the strait. At Chrysopolis, on 18 September, was fought the second and decisive battle of the war. Licinius had mustered considerable forces during the two and a half months that he had held Byzantium. But once again the Labarum prevailed against the images of the gods that Licinius carried into battle. The war was over.

Licinius fled to Nicomedia, whence he sent his wife Constantia to beg her half-brother for his life. Constantine agreed to spare him, and also his colleague Martinianus, and Licinius was received with some graciousness, being invited to dine with his conqueror. He was then conveyed to Thessalonica, where he was to be interned, while Martinianus was removed to Cappadocia. But neither he nor his colleague were long allowed to survive their defeat. An ecclesiastical historian, writing over a century later, declares that Licinius recruited some barbarians and attempted with their aid to regain power, but less biased authorities give no reason for his execution save

Constantine's fear that he might, like old Maximian, aspire to power once more. Eusebius describes Licinius' end with an uncharacteristic brevity and vagueness which are sure proof that it was not creditable to his hero.

9 The Arian and Melitian Controversies

One of Constantine's first acts after his victory was to issue a constitution to his new subjects, remedying all the injuries and losses which had been inflicted on individual Christians and on the churches during the persecutions. In the preamble the Emperor, in his usual turgid and involved style, points the moral of his victory. 'Who,' he rhetorically asks,

could obtain any good who neither recognizes God the author of good things nor will pay Him proper reverence? The facts attest my words. If anyone will run back in his mind over the years which have passed from long ago until now, and will survey the past in his imagination, he will find that all who laid a just and good foundation to their actions advanced their undertakings to a good end and gathered sweet fruit from a sweet root. . . . But all who dishonoured and neglected justice and knew not the Supreme Power, but dared to subject its faithful followers to injury and irremediable penalties, and did not think themselves wretched in that they inflicted penalties for such a cause, and deem happy and blessed them who maintained their reverence for the Supreme Power even in such extremity – their armies have many of them fallen and many turned to flight, and all their array of war has ended in shameful defeat.

Constantine next turns the tables on the pagans by laying the wars, famines and other ills for which the Christians were popularly blamed at the door of the persecutors, who, he proclaims, 'have not only endured misery in this life, but have before their eyes a more grievous fear of the places of punishment beneath the earth'.

Finally, he turns to his own part in the drama:

When such grievous impiety controls human affairs and the commonwealth is in danger of utter destruction as by some plague and has need of much health-giving care, what alleviation does the Divinity devise, what rescue from our danger? And we must regard as altogether divine that which alone and really exists and whose power endures through all time. It is not vainglorious to acknowledge and boast of the beneficence of the Supreme Power. He sought out and judged fitting for His own purpose my service, starting from the sea which laps distant Britain and from those quarters where the sun is commanded by an ordinance of fate to set, thrusting aside by some mightier power all the dangers that beset me, that the human race might be recalled to the worship of the august law, schooled by my agency, and that the blessed faith might be increased under the guidance of the Supreme Power. Never can I ungratefully forget the gratitude that I owe; believing this to be the noblest service, this the gift granted to me, I advanced to the regions of the East, which, consumed by more grievous ills, called aloud for the greater healing care at my hands.

Constantine proceeds to enumerate in detail the measures of redress which he had enacted. Exiles were to return to their homes, and their confiscated property to be restored. Those who had been enrolled on city councils were to be released. Those who had been deported to islands – commonly used as penal settlements – were to return. Persons condemned to the mines or to forced labour on public works were to be set free and recover their previous status. Soldiers and civil servants who had resigned their posts rather than abjure their faith were given the choice of reinstatement or of honourable discharge. Persons who had been condemned to work as slaves of the Treasury in the state weaving establishments were to recover their freedom. The property of those who had been executed, or condemned *in absentia* and since died, was to go to their next of kin, or failing them to their local church; those who had acquired their properties by sale or grant were ordered to surrender them without compensation forthwith. The corporate property of the churches was to be similarly restored, and the graves of the martyrs were to be made over to them.

Constantine might reasonably have hoped that, having righted the wrongs which the worshippers of the Supreme Power had suffered, he could henceforth rest from his labours, secure in'the divine favour. He even hoped, through the aid of Eastern bishops, to solve the intractable problem of the Donatists, which still marred the unity of the Church and might bring down the wrath of God upon His servant. But he had no sooner set foot in Nicomedia than he learned that the Church in his new dominions was riven by an even more widespread controversy, which, starting from a dispute between Alexander, bishop of Alexandria, and Arius, one of his priests, had embroiled the bishops of every province from Libya and Egypt to Bithynia and Thrace.

Arius, the author of the trouble, is known to us only from the accounts of his enemies; and from the fact that they never impugn his moral character, it may be inferred that he was of blameless life. He was, when the controversy opened, already an elderly man, the second in seniority of the twenty-three priests of Alexandria. He is described as very tall, and he affected an ascetic dress, consisting of a sleeveless tunic and a half-length cloak. During his youth he had been a pupil of the celebrated Christian philosopher, Lucian of Antioch, who had carried on the tradition of the great Origen. Origen's Christian Platonism had carried the intellectuals of the Church by storm, and for a while pupils of his school had dominated Christian thought, but even Origen himself had been viewed with suspicion by simple believers, and his successors had drifted yet further from the faith of the common man in the pursuit of their philosophical speculations: Lucian had, during the greater part of his career, been disowned by the successive bishops of Antioch. Arius carried this tendency to its extreme. His surviving writings display no religious feeling and a somewhat offensive intellectual arrogance. He argues from purely philosophical premises, and by clever deduction reaches neat theological conclusions. Nevertheless, he might have pursued his speculations undisturbed but for his exorbitant vanity, which hankered for an admiring audience, so much so that, not content with his regular congregation, he worked up his doctrines in popular ballad verse in order to appeal to the masses.

It is fortunately not necessary for the purpose of this work to explain his doctrines. It may suffice to say that starting from the Platonic premise that God is the eternal and unknowable monad, he deduced that the Son cannot be in the same sense God. He was created or begotten before all ages, it is true, but was nevertheless posterior to the Father, who was not always a Father. He further argued that the Father, since his own being is indivisible, must have created the Son out of nothing. These views shocked a number of the Alexandrian clergy, including the senior priest, Colluthus, and the bishop Alexander was at length moved to intervene. Two debates were held, in which Arius, in the heat of argument, expressed his theological paradoxes in a yet more extreme form, and Alexander was forced to take the serious step of convening a council of bishops. About a hundred bishops from the provinces subject to Alexandria attended, and with two dissentients, Secundus of Ptolemais and Theonas of Marmarice, both from the province of Libya, from which Arius came, condemned the new doctrine, and excommunicated Arius and his adherents.

Arius now appealed to his old fellow student at Lucian's school, Eusebius, who had become bishop of Berytus (Beirut) in Phoenicia, and had then migrated to Nicomedia; as bishop of the city where the Emperor normally resided, he was politically an important figure. The letter is worth reproducing, since it is typical of the man:

To my beloved lord, the faithful man of God, the orthodox Eusebius, Arius, who is persecuted unjustly by the Pope Alexander for the sake of the all-conquering faith which you too champion, sends greetings in the Lord.

Since my father Ammonius is going to Nicomedia, I think it proper and necessary to pay my respects to you through him, and at the same time to inform you, in view of your inborn love and affection for your brothers in God and his Christ, that the bishop is assaulting and persecuting us greatly and employing every device against us: so that he has expelled us from the city as atheists because we do not agree with him when he says publicly, 'Always God, always the Son. At the same time the Father, at the same time the Son. The Son coexists ingenerately with God, he is ever begotten, he is ingenerately begotten. Neither in thought, nor by a single moment does God precede the Son. Always God, always the Son. The Son is of God himself.' And when your brother, Eusebius of Caesarea, and Theodotus and Paulinus, and Athanasius and Gregory and Aetius, in fact, all the bishops of the East, declare that God is without beginning pre-existent to the Son, they have become anathema: except only Philogonius and Hellanicus and Macarius, uneducated heretics, who say the Son is an eructation or a projection or co-ingenerate.

We cannot endure to hear these impieties, if the heretics threaten us with a thousand deaths. What we say and believe we have taught and still teach: that the Son is not ingenerate or a part of the ingenerate in any way, nor from any underlying matter. But that he came into being by God's will and counsel before all times and ages, full God only begotten and

unchangeable: and before he was begotten, or created or determined or founded, he did not exist. For he was not ingenerate. We are persecuted because we said: the Son has a
beginning; God is without a beginning. For that we are persecuted and because we said that he is from nothing. So we said
because he is not part of God, and not from any underlying
matter. For that we are persecuted. You know the rest. Farewell in the Lord, remembering our tribulations, fellow student
of Lucian, truly Eusebius [a play on the meaning of 'Eusebius'
– pious].

Eusebius replied encouragingly to his old friend:

Your views are right; pray that all may believe as you do. It is
plain to anyone that that which is made does not exist before it
comes into being: that which comes into being has a beginning
of its being.

Arius soon went to Nicomedia himself, and as the controversy had spread beyond Egypt, Alexander felt obliged
to circularize the bishops of the East, informing them of
the fact that he had excommunicated Arius and his associates and stating his grounds for having done so. He
explained that he had hoped by maintaining silence to let
the evil die a natural death without infecting others.

But since Eusebius, the present bishop of Nicomedia, who
thinks that the affairs of the Church are in his hands, because
when he left Berytus and set his cap at Nicomedia his conduct
was not censured, champions these apostates, and has tried to
write everywhere on their behalf, in order to drag ignorant
persons into this latest anti-Christian heresy, I have found it
necessary, knowing what is written in the law, to break my
silence and to inform you all, so that you may know who the
apostates are and the wretched utterances of their heresy, and
may pay no attention if Eusebius writes to you.

It is evident that Alexander was stung to the quick by
Eusebius' action in taking up the cause of his rebel subjects.

Eusebius retorted by summoning a council of bishops in his own province of Bithynia, which approved Arius' doctrine, and circularized all bishops, urging them to receive Arius into communion and bring pressure on Alexander to take him back. At the same time, Arius and his followers wrote to Alexander, giving a formal statement of their faith, opening with the rather provocative words, 'This is our ancestral faith, which we learned from you also, blessed Pope.' Alexander countered this attack on his orthodoxy by circulating a full statement of his faith, and asking for signatures; he eventually collected about two hundred. A regular war of pamphlets now began, of which sundry fragments have come down to us. Arius travelled to Palestine and enlisted the interest of the other Eusebius, bishop of Caesarea, who summoned a council of Palestinian bishops. This council also approved Arius' faith, and passed a resolution that he should be reinstated in his parish church of Alexandria, but should submit to Alexander and seek to be reconciled with him.

Arius and his supporters appear to have acted on this resolution, for Alexander, in a voluminous letter to his namesake of Byzantium, complains bitterly that Arius and Achillas, one of his supporters, 'have built themselves robbers' caves and unceasingly hold conventicles in them by night and by day,' and 'raise riots and persecutions against me every day, at one time concocting lawsuits through the agency of undisciplined females whom they have deceived, at another bringing discredit on Christianity by making their young women parade around the streets in a disorderly fashion' – Arius seems to have had great success with women; he is elsewhere recorded to have had seven hundred holy virgins among his adherents.

It was probably at this stage that Constantine intervened. His initial reaction was that of the plain man. He could not understand the metaphysical subtleties on which the dispute centred, and, regarding them as unimportant, he urged the two disputants to agree to differ. He accordingly drafted a letter to Alexander and Arius jointly, and entrusted it to Hosius, the bishop of Corduba, who remained his unofficial ecclesiastical adviser.

In his opening paragraphs Constantine solemnly declares that the main object of his recent campaign against Licinius was to heal the Donatist controversy.

For an intolerable madness having gripped all Africa owing to those who dared with senseless levity to rend the worship of the peoples into separate sects, wishing to check this plague, I could find no other adequate cure for the trouble save to expel the common enemy of the world, who opposed his lawless will to your sacred councils, and send some of you to aid in bringing concord to the rival disputants.

He goes on to enlarge on the high hopes he entertained of the East as the original home of Christianity, on his bitter disappointment on hearing that the East was yet more divided than the West, and on his surprise on discovering the 'extremely trifling' cause of the dispute.

This I understand, was the cause of the present dissension. You, Alexander, asked your priests what each of them thought about some passage in the scriptures, or rather about some frivolous question, and you, Arius, imprudently made an answer which should never have been conceived at all, or if conceived should have been committed to silence. Hence discord came between you, and the holy people were rent between you and parted from the harmony of the general body. Therefore let each of you, sharing an equal spirit of concession, accept the just advice that your fellow servant offers you. And what is that? You ought not to have raised such questions at all, and if they were raised, not to have answered. For such investigations, which no legal necessity imposes, but the frivolity of an idle hour provokes, we should, even if they are made for the sake of a philosophic exercise, lock up within our hearts and not bring forward into public gatherings or entrust imprudently to the ears of the people.... To remind your understanding by a a small example, you know, I take it, that even philosophers all agree on one doctrine, and often, when they disagree on some part of their arguments, though they are divided by the keenness of their intellect, agree with one another again in the unity of their belief. If this is so, how much more should we, the servants of the great God, maintain harmony with one another?

Constantine ends with a passionate appeal:

Give me back peaceful nights and days without care that I too may keep some pleasure in the pure light and the joy of a tranquil life henceforth.... That you may understand the excess of my sorrow, yesterday when I set foot in the city of Nicomedia, I was pressing immediately to the East in my imagination. But as I hastened to you and was all but with you, the news of this trouble reined back my purpose, that I might not be compelled to see with my eyes what I felt I could not bear to hear with my ears. Open to me by your agreement the road to the East, which you have closed by your mutual discord.

Hosius seems soon to have discovered that the controversy was too embittered to be solved by the Emperor's advice to agree to differ. He also discovered that the Arian dispute was not the only conflict in the Church of Egypt: there were two other schisms, one of recent date and minor importance, the other of considerable extent and dating back nearly twenty years. The lesser trouble had been caused by Colluthus, the senior priest of Alexandria, who had recently usurped the rank of bishop and ordained some priests. The origin of this schism is unknown, but Colluthus was a violent opponent of Arius, and it may be that he considered that Alexander's attitude was not firm enough. Hosius was able to quell this sedition, summoning and presiding over a local council of a hundred bishops which reduced Colluthus to the priesthood again. Colluthus' followers, however, remained unconvinced, and such was their bitterness that they stoned the statue of the new emperor – an act of high treason.

The other schism proved more intractable. It went back to the early days of the great persecution, and the first picture that we have of it shows a number of Egyptian bishops, including Peter of Alexandria and Melitius of Lycopolis, in prison together. A dispute arises on the treatment of those who have lapsed in the persecution. Melitius stands for a rigorous policy: the lapsed must wait till the persecution is over before they are even admitted to repentance; otherwise, what incentive is there to resist the government's orders? Furthermore, lapsed clergy must never be permitted to resume their sacred functions. Peter urges a more lenient treatment, for fear lest the lapsed should be discouraged and fall away altogether, if they are given no hope of being reconciled with the Church. The dispute becomes more and more exacerbated, until at length Peter hangs a curtain across the middle of the room and orders all who refuse to accept his ruling to leave his half of the prison. The majority of the bishops move to Melitius' end of the prison, and the two parties cease to be on speaking terms.

The next event is dated to shortly after Easter, 306. The bishops have by now been released, and Peter issues a series of rulings on the treatment of the lapsed. They are, on the whole, mild. Those who gave way after torture and flogging may be received back into the Church after a further forty days' fast. Those who yielded to imprisonment only must undergo a year of penance; those who yielded to mere threats must repent for an additional three years. Those guilty of evasion, by bribing the officials or getting pagans to impersonate them, are pardoned or let off with light sentences; but owners who made their Christian slaves sacrifice in their place are condemned to three years'

penance. Those who sacrificed but then recanted and confessed the faith are pardoned. So too are those who went
into hiding; spontaneous martyrdoms are, on the other
hand, deprecated. Lapsed clergy are not to be readmitted
to their functions, but clergy who were constrained by
physical violence to go through the motions of sacrifice
are not to be treated as lapsed.

The publication of these rulings would seem to have
driven Melitius into formal revolt. At the next stage that
we can trace in the controversy four Egyptian bishops in
prison write a letter of protest to Melitius, who they have
heard is making ordinations outside his own diocese, dis-
regarding the obedience he owes to Peter and the tribulations and imprisonment of the writers: they were soon
afterwards executed. Melitius ignored this appeal, which
was couched in polite and conciliatory language, and proceeded to visit Alexandria, taking advantage of the fact
that Peter was hiding in the country. There he managed to
discover the hiding-places of the priests whom Peter had
left in charge and incited them to disaffection; he was
then arrested, and while in prison consecrated a bishop.
Peter now excommunicated Melitius provisionally, till it
should be possible to hold a council. Melitius was next
condemned to forced labour in the copper mines at Phaeno
in southern Palestine, and on his journey thither he ordained more priests, and in the mines themselves another
bishop. The schism was now complete: at Phaeno itself
the Christian convicts built themselves two rival churches,
one labelled 'the Catholic Church' and the other 'the
Church of the Martyrs'. Melitius eventually returned to
Egypt, probably under the general amnesty issued by Galerius shortly before his death in 311. Despite the martyrdom of Peter eighteen months later, the breach between
the Catholic Church and the Church of the Martyrs remained unhealed, and the quarrel persisted through the

episcopates of Achillas and Alexander. Melitius seems to have gained ground steadily, for his Church boasted by now some thirty-five bishops.

On receiving Hosius' report, Constantine decided that a council was needed to solve these two conflicts, and he issued invitations to the bishops to an assembly at Ancyra. It is not certain how comprehensive a council Constantine envisaged at this stage: it was certainly to be a large gathering, and invitations must have been issued to all bishops in Licinius' former dominions, who were already involved in the dispute, but the Emperor does not as yet seem to have thought of bringing in those of the West.

On 20 December 324 Philogonius, the bishop of Antioch, died. He had been a strong supporter of Alexander, and it was clearly important, in the interests of his party, that this key bishopric should be held by a sound man. Hosius, who appears to have been convinced by Alexander's argument, forthwith convened a council from all the provinces subject to Antioch, from Cilicia and Mesopotamia to Palestine. The council, which was probably 'packed', was strongly anti-Arian in tone. It rapidly disposed of its official agenda by regulating certain abuses in the Church of Antioch which had arisen in the Licinian persecution, passing a number of resolutions on Church discipline, and electing to the vacant throne of Antioch Eustathius, bishop of Beroea, a rabid anti-Arian; in deference to the Emperor, Eustathius does not seem to have been actually consecrated pending confirmation by his great council. The bishops then proceeded to discuss the doctrinal issue, and compiled a statement of the faith which condemned Arius' views and supported those of Alexander. Growing bolder yet, they condemned the views of three bishops who had supported Arius – Narcissus of Neronias, Theodotus of Laodicea and the learned Eusebius of Caesarea, and excommunicated them provisionally, pending the great Council at Ancyra, by which time they hoped that they would have seen the error of their ways. Finally, they communicated their decisions, including their exposition of the faith and their provisional excommunication of the three dissentients, not only to the Eastern provinces, but to the bishop of Rome, for circularization in the West.

We do not know if Hosius had Constantine's authority for convening the Council of Antioch. He fairly certainly exceeded his instructions in encouraging or allowing the council to pre-judge the issue which was to come before the emperor's great council and to bring the Western Churches into the dispute. Faced with this situation Constantine took a decision which was to form a vital precedent in the relation of State and Church. He would summon a universal council, representative of the whole Church, and he would preside over the council himself. Accordingly he issued the following circular letter to all the bishops:

That there is nothing more precious in my eyes than religion is, I think, clear to all. Whereas it was previously settled that the congress of bishops should be at Ancyra of Galatia, it has now been decided for many reasons that it should meet at the city of Nicaea in Bithynia, both because the bishops from Italy and the other parts of Europe are coming, and because of its pleasant climate, and further in order that I may be near to watch and take part in the proceedings. I therefore inform you, beloved brethren, that I wish you all to meet as soon as possible in the above-mentioned city, Nicaea. Each of you accordingly, regarding his duty, as I have previously said, must without any delay urgently expedite his journey, so that he may personally observe the proceedings of the congress. God will preserve you, beloved brethren.

It is tantalizing that, while we possess the full minutes of the later and less famous Councils of Ephesus and Chalcedon, we have no official record of the proceedings of the first oecumenical congress of the Church, the world famous Council of Nicaea. From official sources we know only the finished results of the Council. We possess the creed or statement of the faith which the bishops drew up and, in various versions, all corrupt and deficient, their signatures to it. We have the twenty canons, or rulings on Church law and discipline, which the Council passed. There is also extant the synodical letter in which the Council officially communicated to the Church of Alexandria those parts of its decisions which especially affected Egypt. And finally we have two letters of Constantine, one addressed especially to the Church of Alexandria, urging a unanimous and hearty acceptance of the Council's creed, and the other communicating to the Churches at large the decision of the Council on the date of Easter.

But for the actual debates we have to rely on fragmentary and *ex parte* statements, some of them made long after the event. Eusebius of Caesarea, who took a leading part in the Council, has left us, in his life of Constantine, which was written some twelve years after the meeting, a vague and rhetorical description of the proceedings, which concentrates on the glamorous externals of the great assembly and draws a discreet veil over its embittered debates. Other writers have preserved a much more interesting document from the pen of Eusebius, the letter which he wrote to his own church at Caesarea immediately after the Council, explaining – or rather explaining away – his acceptance of the creed which he had under pressure signed. Apart from this we have a brief and biased account of the opening debates from that embittered anti-Arian, Eustathius, the recently elected bishop of Antioch. We have also the account given by Athanasius, who attended the Council as one of Alexander's deacons, of the debates over the crucial clauses of the creed: this was written about twenty-five years later and is highly polemical. Finally, we have a letter, written two years after the event, by Eusebius of Nicomedia and Theognius of Nicaea, explaining the line that they took in the final decisions.

We do not even know how many bishops attended. The traditional number of 'the 318 fathers' first becomes current a generation later, and is motivated by a parallelism, dear to the spirit of the age, with the 318 servants of Abraham. Among contemporaries, Eusebius says over 250, Eustathius about 270 – he gives this explicitly as an estimate, stating that he had not counted them – and Constantine 300 and more. The lists of signatures vary in detail, but altogether give no more than 220 odd names; they are, however, certainly defective. Probably Constantine exaggerated, and Eusebius and Eustathius are nearer the mark; the number is surprisingly small.

The response to the Emperor's invitation from the West was negligible; the points at issue were of no interest to Western bishops, and for the most part unintelligible to them, and not even the offer of a free journey to the imperial court tempted them. The bishop of Rome excused himself on the grounds of age and ill-health, but sent two deacons to represent him. The only Italian bishop who attended was Marcus of Calabria. Gaul and the Illyrian provinces were represented by one bishop each. From Africa came Caecilian of Carthage, who was evidently anxious to confirm his title to his see by obtaining tacit or explicit recognition by the great Council. From Britain and from Spain there came no representatives; Hosius of Corduba attended, but as the Emperor's ecclesiastical adviser, in which capacity he took precedence over the delegates of the Pope.

The universal character of the Council was emphasized by the presence of a few bishops from beyond the frontiers of the Empire, two from the Crimea, two from the kingdom of Greater Armenia and one from Persia: these outlandish figures excited general curiosity, and are mentioned by every author who describes the Council, though not unnaturally they took no active part in the proceedings. The great bulk of the Council came from the Greek-speaking provinces of the empire. Among the signatories nineteen are Egyptian bishops, twenty-five from the provinces of the East, and over a hundred from Asia Minor; the Greek-speaking provinces of Europe are more sparsely represented by eleven bishops. The leading scholars and theologians of the East were all present, men such as the two Eusebii, of Caesarea and of Nicomedia, Alexander of Alexandria, Marcellus of Ancyra, Eustathius of Antioch, Paulinus of Tyre. But as was natural in so large a gathering, they were in a small minority. The bulk of the gathering were simple pastors, who would naturally resent any innovation on the faith which they had learned and would have little sympathy with the intellectual paradoxes of Arius. Many could boast of the proud title of confessor, having endured imprisonment, torture and penal servitude for the sake of their faith.

The Council was formally opened on 20 May 325. The bishops were assembled in a great hall of the imperial palace at Nicaea, seated on benches which ran down the length of the room on either side. There was an expectant hush. Presently one of the high imperial officials entered and took his seat, and gradually others trickled in. Then came the great moment: at a given signal the assembly rose, and the Emperor entered, in his full imperial robes of purple decked with gold and precious stones, but without his usual bodyguard, attended only by a few members of his council. Eusebius describes with what modest hesitancy and blushing humility the Emperor walked forward with downcast eyes to the small gilded chair which had been placed for him in the centre of the room, and how he refused to be seated until the bishops indicated their assent: this was a striking contrast to the imperial consistory, where the members of the imperial council had to stand in the Emperor's presence. The bishop who occupied the first seat on the right-hand side – we do not know who he was, Eustathius and the two Eusebii all being candidates for the honour – then delivered a speech of thanks and welcome to the Emperor. When he ceased, all eyes were turned on Constantine and a profound silence enveloped them all.

Constantine rose and made a short speech in Latin – not that he was unfamiliar with Greek, but that he wished to mark that this was an official occasion by employing for its formal inauguration the official language of the Empire. The speech followed the lines that were to be expected, deploring internecine strife within the Church as a greater disaster than war or invasion, and urging the assembled bishops to win the favour of God and earn the Emperor's gratitude by resolving all discord and achieving harmony.

An interpreter read a Greek translation of the speech, and the Emperor opened the debate. On the procedure and course of the debate there has been and still is much dispute, but certain points are clear. During the crucial debate on the creed the Emperor was himself in the chair, and took an active part in guiding the proceedings. The rules of procedure in Church councils appear to have been modelled on those of the Roman senate and of town councils, and in these the presiding magistrate played a more positive rôle than does a chairman of a meeting today: he posed the issue, asked the members severally for their views, intervened himself in the debate, supporting or opposing the views expressed by members, and selected which of the motions proposed should be put to the house. Eusebius makes it clear that Constantine made full use of his position. He praises his patience and good temper in allowing all sides to express their views without hurry, but he especially emphasizes his active efforts to resolve difficulties and promote concord, by stressing certain points brought up by either side, commending those who spoke well, reinforcing the arguments of some and reproving others.

Constantine's general line is tolerably clear, both from his previous pronouncements on the controversy and his policy subsequent to the Council. He was no metaphysician, and regarded the dispute as unnecessary and irreverent: on the other hand, he had a deep-seated conviction that any division within the Church was an offence to the Supreme Power and might bring down His wrath on the Empire and on himself, to whose care the Empire had been committed. What Constantine wanted, therefore, was an inclusive formula which all could accept. Acceptance of this formula would be a qualification for Church membership, and would not preclude differences of opinion on its interpretation or on points not covered by it. Among the bishops there were many, no doubt, who agreed with the Emperor, but there was also a strong party which regarded Arius' views as blasphemous and were determined to frame a formula which should exclude them. The majority of the Arians seem to have been willing to accept a loosely framed formula which would admit their beliefs without imposing them on others.

The three accounts of the debate which we possess are very different, and it is difficult to see whether they represent successive stages in it, or are variant versions, distorted by the authors' prejudices, of the same events. According to Eustathius, Eusebius – he does not indicate which – brought forward a document which, on being read to the assembly, caused immeasurable distress to the audience and indelible shame to its author on account of the perversity of its doctrine. The document was torn to pieces in the sight of all, but at this stage certain persons, on the pretext of peace, plotted to silence all the ablest speakers. Eusebius of Caesarea describes how he brought forward the traditional creed of his Church; that it was universally approved, especially by the Emperor, who recommended its acceptance with certain amendments; that he, after grave doubts, accepted the amendments in deference to the Emperor; and that the revised creed was accepted by the Council. Athanasius describes the bishops amending a creed in such a way as to exclude Arian beliefs, and being forced to use new and disputable terms in order to achieve their object.

It has been generally believed that Eustathius is describing an early stage in the proceedings, when Eusebius of Nicomedia, Arius' chief advocate, brought forward a frankly Arian creed, which was rejected by an overwhelming majority. It seems odd, however, that Constantine should have permitted the debate to become exacerbated at so early a stage, and odder still that Eusebius, who was, if anything, a good tactician, should have courted defeat by openly espousing an extremist statement; he knew that Alexander had behind him a solid phalanx of Egyptians and that Eustathius could rely on the large block of Oriental bishops who had met at Antioch. It may be, therefore, that Eustathius and Eusebius are describing the same event from their respective angles. Eustathius, a rabid anti-Arian and bitter enemy of Eusebius of Caesarea, regarded his vaguely phrased creed – which would have left a loophole for Arius – as an heretical document, and describes the dissatisfaction of his party with its terms, and their resentment at not being allowed by the Emperor – the guarded phrase 'certain persons' clearly alludes to him – to propose a thoroughgoing anti-Arian formula. Eusebius, on the other hand, exaggerated the welcome given to his creed, and very seriously minimizes the degree to which it was reshaped before it was accepted.

If this view be accepted, Constantine called upon Eusebius of Caesarea, whose learning he greatly respected, and whom he regarded as a middle of the road theologian – as indeed he was – to propose a creed. Eusebius produced the traditional baptismal creed of Caesarea, which runs as follows:

As we have received from the bishops who preceded us, both in our first instruction and when we received baptism, and as we have learned from the divine Scriptures, and as we believed and taught in the office of priest, and also in that of bishop, so believing also at the time present, we report to you our faith, as follows:

We believe in One God, the Father Almighty, the Maker of all things visible and invisible. And in One Lord Jesus Christ, the Word of God, God from God, Light from Light, Life from Life, only-begotten Son, first-born of all creation, begotten from the Father before all the ages, by Whom also all things were made, Who for our salvation was made flesh and lived among men, and suffered, and rose again the third day, and ascended to the Father, and will come again in glory to judge the living and the dead. And we believe also in One Holy Spirit:

Believing each of these to be and to exist, the Father truly Father, and the Son truly Son, and the Holy Ghost truly Holy Ghost, as also our Lord, sending forth His own disciples to preach said, 'Go teach all nations, baptizing them in the Name of the Father, and of the Son, and of the Holy Ghost.' Concerning whom we confidently affirm that so we hold, and so we think, and so we have held long ago, and we maintain this faith unto death, anathematizing every godless heresy.

It was an impeccable document, hallowed by tradition, strictly scriptural, and the Emperor accepted it warmly. The members of the Council, when asked their opinion, expressed their approval: they could hardly do otherwise, for there was nothing wrong with it so far as it went. But to the large group who wished to condemn Arianism, it was profoundly unsatisfactory, because any Arian could accept it. 'God from God' might seem to be a difficulty to them, but Arius had never denied that the Son was God, and the phrase, he could argue, expressed no unique relation between the Son and the Father, for according to the scriptures all things are from God.

Various amendments were proposed. Some suggested that the Son should be described as 'the True Power and Image of the Father', others as 'in all things exactly like the Father', or as 'unalterable', as 'God without division'. But to their exasperation the Arian bishops, after exchanging winks and whispering to each other, blandly accepted these amendments; after all, they argued among themselves, 'Man is the image and glory of God', so why not the Son, and as for 'power', the caterpillar and the locust are called in scripture 'the power of the Lord'.

It was at this stage that Constantine dropped his bombshell on the Council. He suggested that the relation of the Son to the Father might be expressed by the word *homoousios*, of one essence. Eusebius is explicit that the Emperor himself proposed this term, even if Athanasius, writing twenty-five years later, preferred to forget this embarrassing fact, and attribute its introduction to the bishops at large.

The earlier history of this famous word is somewhat obscure, but some significant facts are certain. The opponents of Arius had never hitherto used it: it figures neither in Alexander's statement of the faith, which was so widely circulated and received so many signatures, nor in the creed devised by the Council of Antioch in 324, both specifically anti-Arian documents. And the anti-Arian party had good reason to fight shy of it. The great Dionysius, bishop of Alexandria during the Decian and Valerian persecutions, had roundly condemned it in his controversy with the Monarchian bishops of Libya, and though, in deference to his namesake of Rome, he had later been obliged to admit its orthodoxy, he had done so with obvious reluctance, and with careful reservations as to its interpretation. Rather later, in 268, an important council of the Orient had, in condemning Paul of Samosata, explicitly anathematized the term. How widely the Homoousion was disliked in the East is also shown by its subsequent history. So soon as Constantine was dead – for no one dared to touch his creed during his lifetime – creed after creed was worked out to eliminate the hateful word, and this by bishops who were for the most part not Arian; it was not till half a century had passed that the Homoousion had become sufficiently familiar to be generally acceptable, and by this time its meaning had been considerably modified by discussion and interpretation.

But if to the general body of learned opinion in the East, which was based on Origen's metaphysics, the Homoousion was profoundly distasteful, it had been accepted doctrine in the unphilosophic West for a century or more. Pope Dionysius had, as we have seen, compelled his namesake and contemporary of Alexandria to accept the term, and before him Tertullian had used terminology that clearly implies it. It may be also that among plain believers in the East the term was accepted, though there is no positive evidence of this.

The conclusion is inescapable that Constantine was relying on the advice of his regular ecclesiastical adviser, the Spanish bishop Hosius, when he proposed the term. Hosius, no doubt, acted in all innocence, imagining that the word was generally accepted as orthodox; he may even, as some ecclesiastical historians writing over a century later state, have consulted Alexander beforehand and received his consent; for Alexander could justify his acceptance of the term by the precedent of his predecessor Dionysius. And from his point of view the Homoousion had one great point in its favour. Arius had, in his formal declaration of faith, condemned it as Manichaean, about the worst thing he could say of any doctrine, and could not possibly accept it.

The anti-Arian party in the Council therefore accepted the Emperor's amendment, supported no doubt by many simple-minded bishops who were unaware of its theological implications. And having got the ball at their feet, they proceeded to rewrite Eusebius' creed, not merely inserting the clause 'of one essence with the Father', but introducing the explanatory phrase 'that is, of the essence of the Father' after 'begotten of the Father'. They also insisted on a specific statement that the Son was 'begotten, not made'. Not content with this, they added to the positive statement of the faith a number of anathemas condemning specific Arian statements such as, 'he was created out of nothing' and 'before he was begotten he was not', since they could now argue that the creed implicitly contained these anathemas.

How profoundly distressing these changes were to Eusebius of Caesarea can be seen from the letter which he hastened to write to his Church. It is a pathetic document, equivocal to the point of dishonesty. He had evidently expected, and perhaps had indiscreetly let it be known, that he was to be triumphantly vindicated from the slur which the Council of Antioch had laid upon his ortho-doxy, and that the creed of Caesarea was to be accepted by the Universal Church. He begins by asking his people not to believe alarmist rumours which may have trickled through before hearing his own full statement. He then tells how he read his creed to the Council and how no ob-jection could be raised to it, and how the Emperor himself praised its orthodoxy and urged all the bishops to subscribe to it with the single addition of the Homoousion. Next Eusebius cites the creed of the Council, which in fact contains many other changes, and tries to justify his acceptance of them, insisting that he has examined their implications with care. 'Of the essence of the Father' meant, he explains, merely that the Son was 'of the Father', not a part of him. 'Begotten not made' only emphasized that the Son was not created in the same sense that the world was created, but was brought into being in a manner beyond human comprehension. As for the Homoousion, the Em-peror himself had explained that it did not imply any division of the essence of the Father, or any change or alteration in his power, but merely emphasized that the Son had no resemblance to created things, but was like the Father alone, and was of no other substance but of the Father. He was consoled by the fact that learned and dis-tinguished bishops and writers had used the term in times past. As for the anathemas, the phrases used were unscrip-tural and he had never used them himself. The statement 'he was not before he was begotten' was clearly false, since the Son had existed before his generation in the flesh, and the Emperor had further argued that he existed potentially before the divine generation.

It thus appears that the anti-Arian party exploited the

Emperor's authority to the full to force through a creed impossible for Arius to accept, not caring if it alienated many others. The Emperor wanted unanimity, and now that a formula apparently satisfactory to the great majority had emerged, he used all his influence to persuade the remaining doubters to conform. He probably did not realize how paralysing an effect his imperial presence had on free discussion, and how far the apparently willing consent of the great majority was due to deference to his authority. Nor did he probably realize that he was forcing on a number of bishops a doctrine to which they could not conscientiously subscribe. He had been told on the best of authority that the term 'Homoousion' was correct, and in any case unanimity was more important than metaphysical minutiae. So Eusebius of Caesarea, after long wrestles with his conscience, signed. Even Eusebius of Nicomedia and Theognius of Nicaea, who had gone much further in accepting Arius' position, signed in the end. Finally, only two bishops stood out, Arius' old supporters Secundus of Ptolemais and Theonas of Marmarice. The Council proceeded to excommunicate these two as well as Arius himself, and to order their deprivation. The Emperor followed up this sentence by ordering their deportation from Egypt. Against this sentence of the Council, Eusebius of Nicomedia and Theognius of Nicaea rebelled; they were willing to agree that the doctrines condemned by the Council were false, but they denied that their friend had held such views and refused to concur with his excommunication. For this contumacy they were apparently excommunicated themselves, but not deprived; they were probably given time to reconsider their decision.

We do not know how the decision of the Council on the Melitian schism was reached, but it can probably be regarded as Constantine's own handiwork, for it cannot have pleased Alexander – Athanasius later regarded it as

profoundly unsatisfactory – and the Melitians were a local
sect without any external backing. Constantine had evidently learnt wisdom from his experience with the Donatists, A judicial decision that one side was in the wrong was
in such a case useless, for the defeated party only defied it
and the schism was accentuated by any attempt to use
force. The Council therefore was persuaded to take a very
lenient view. Melitius himself was to retain the title only
of bishop, being forbidden to exercise any episcopal functions, but the other Melitian bishops, on confirmation by
Alexander, were to retain their functions, ranking as junior to Alexander's and not being able to make any
ordinations without Alexander's agreement; as vacancies
occurred they might, with Alexander's consent, replace their
catholic opposite numbers. The compromise was complicated, but might have been worked with goodwill on both
sides. Unfortunately that goodwill was lacking.

The other main topic on the agenda, the date of Easter,
was probably placed there by the Emperor, who attached
great importance to the externals of religious observance,
and must have been shocked to find different Churches
celebrating the feast on different days: the anomaly had
been brought to his attention over ten years before by a
canon of the Council of Arles. The question is highly technical, and it may suffice to give a brief outline only. Easter
is based on the Jewish Passover, which was celebrated on
the fourteenth or full moon, of the lunar month Nisan:
this lunar month of course did not occur at a fixed date in
the solar calendar, but was kept by intercalation about the
spring equinox. The first dispute arose when some Churches kept Easter on the full moon, irrespective of the day
of the week, and others on the Sunday following; there was
a further refinement of this dispute if the full moon happened to fall on a Sunday, some Churches, to avoid celebrating Easter on the Jewish Passover, postponing the feast

for a week. The next issue was which full moon should govern the date of the feast. Some Churches accepted the Jewish 14 Nisan, others argued, that as the Jews sometimes celebrated Passover before the vernal equinox, in some years two passovers were celebrated in the solar year (from equinox to equinox) and in some years none at all. Easter, they declared, must be calculated from the first full moon after the spring equinox. This again raised astronomical and mathematical difficulties, for the Churches had diverse views as to which day of March was the true equinox, and used diverse cycles for calculating the future dates of the full moon.

The Council decided in principle for uniformity, confirming the practice of Rome, Italy, Africa, Spain, Gaul, Britain, Egypt, Greece, the Asiatic and Pontic dioceses and Cilicia, and ordering the other Churches, presumably those of Syria and Palestine and the Illyrian provinces, to conform. This decision was not satisfactory, since in point of fact Alexandria and Rome, which were followed by the Eastern and Western Churches respectively, had different dates for the equinox and different cycles: perhaps the Council was unaware of these abstruse mathematical problems, or perhaps it was reluctant to make a decision between two such important sees.

Constantine himself communicated to the Churches the Council's decision on this point. His letter is mainly notable for its strongly anti-Semitic flavour. 'It seems unworthy', he writes, 'to calculate this most holy feast according to the customs of the Jews, who, having stained their hands with lawless crime, are naturally, in their foulness, blind in soul'; and again, 'What right opinions can they have, who, after the murder of the Lord, went out of their minds and are led, not by reason, but by uncontrolled passion?' The main object of the reform is represented as being to sever 'all communication with the perjury of the

Jews'. The day on which a Roman emperor was converted to Christianity proved an unfortunate one for the Jewish people. From henceforth the contemptuous toleration which the Roman government had hitherto shown towards Judaism changed slowly but steadily into hostility, culminating in the drastic penal laws of the most orthodox emperor, Justinian.

A ruling of the Council on 'those who call themselves Pure' is probably also due to Constantine's influence. 'The Pure', commonly known from their founder as Novatians, were a rigorist sect who held that there was no pardon for any mortal sin after baptism, and therefore refused communion to Christians who had lapsed in persecutions. They also regarded second marriages as mortal sin. Constantine appears to have had a considerable respect for their leader Bishop Acesius, whom he summoned to Nicaea. Acesius' doctrinal views were unassailable: when Constantine, so the story goes, proudly showed him the creed worked out by the Council, Acesius, after reading it through, replied briefly: 'There is nothing new in the decision of the Council; that is our tradition from apostolic times.' On the Emperor's asking why he separated himself from the common body of the Church, Acesius explained the stern rule of his sect, which dated from the Decian persecution. The Emperor replied jocosely: 'Put up a ladder, Acesius, and climb into heaven alone'; but he seems to have retained a lurking fear that the old man might be right. The ruling of the Council on those Novatian clergy who wished to return to the Church was on similar lines to that which regulated the Melitian schism. They were, after confirmation, to retain their orders, provided that they signed a declaration that they would communicate with the twice-married and with the lapsed. In villages and cities where there were no Catholic clergy they were to retain their positions: where there were both a Catholic and a Novatian bishop in one community, the Novatian might, with the Catholic's consent, keep the honorary rank of bishop, and must at all events be allowed to exercise the functions of a 'country bishop' or at least a priest. The Paulianists, or followers of Paul of Samosata, who had been condemned for heresy in 268, had less generous treatment; they had to submit to rebaptism, and their clergy were to be reinstated only after searching inquisitions into their fitness.

The other canons of the Council dealt with a variety of points which happened to arise. Several reflect the growing organization of the Church. Bishops must be consecrated by at least three bishops of the province, with the written consent of the others and the confirmation of the metropolitan. Two provincial councils were to be held annually, in spring and in autumn, to review the cases of persons who had been excommunicated by any of the bishops and to decide on a uniform policy. Bishops and clergy were not to migrate from the Church to which they had been ordained and seek promotion elsewhere. The special rights of the see of Alexandria over all bishops of Libya and Egypt were confirmed – Alexander no doubt demanded this reaffirmation of his authority to enable him to deal firmly with the Melitians – and the similar but less far-reaching rights of the sees of Rome, Antioch and the other great metropolitans over groups of provinces were acknowledged. The see of Aelia (the name which Hadrian had given to Jerusalem) was recognized as possessing special honour, without prejudice to the jurisdiction of its metropolitan see, Caesarea.

Several canons deal with the Licinian persecution, condemning to twelve years of penance those who had lapsed without compulsion or confiscation of their goods or danger, and to thirteen years civil servants and soldiers who had initially resigned their posts rather than sacrifice, and had later, 'returning like dogs to their own vomit', recovered their posts by bribery. The lapsed were to receive last communion on the point of death, but if they subsequently recovered were to be excluded once more. Other canons dealt with more ordinary matters of Church discipline. The precipitate ordination of converts immediately after baptism was condemned; the ordination of those guilty of serious sins was declared invalid; eunuchs were admitted to orders only if castrated by their doctors for medical reasons, or by their owners, or by barbarians against their will. The practice of kneeling at prayer on Sundays and between Easter and Whitsun was condemned. Deacons were reproved for their presumption in distributing the eucharist to the priests and even themselves communicating before the priests and the bishop. Priests were prohibited from practising usury: it had come to the knowledge of the council that some had been charging 1 per cent per month or demanding the repayment of loans with a bonus of 50 per cent. Bishops, priests and deacons were not to have female companions to keep house for them, other than their mothers, sisters or aunts.

One motion was defeated: that the married clergy should separate from their wives. It was strongly opposed by the Egyptian bishop, Paphnutius, who firmly maintained that marriage was an honourable estate and that the proposed rule would put too great a strain on human frailty, especially that of the abandoned wives. Paphnutius was a notable confessor – a blinded eye and a limping leg bore witness to his steadfastness under the persecution of Maximin – and the Council deferred to him and resolved to maintain the old rule which forbade marriage subsequent to ordination.

At length the deliberations of the Council were finished, and to celebrate their triumphant conclusion Constantine invited all the bishops to take part in the festivities of his

Vicennalia, the twentieth anniversary of his accession, which happened to fall at this time. Eusebius depicts their emotions as they passed through the anterooms of the Imperial Palace, lined with guards standing with drawn swords, and were admitted to the inmost hall, where some had the honour of reclining at the Emperor's own table. 'It felt', he writes, 'as if we were imagining a picture of the Kingdom of Christ, and that what was happening was no reality, but a dream.'

The Aftermath of
the Council

Constantine was justly proud of the great Council which he had summoned and in whose deliberations he had himself played so decisive a rôle. 'At the suggestion of God,' he wrote to the Church of Alexandria, 'I assembled at the city of Nicaea the greatest number of bishops, with whom I, as one of you, exceedingly glad to be your fellow-servant, myself undertook the examination of the truth'; and again, addressing the Churches, 'The majority of the bishops being assembled, I too was myself present as one of you, for I would not deny my greatest cause for pleasure, that I am your fellow-servant.'

The creed was to his mind a final and inspired statement of the truth: 'For the decision of three hundred bishops must be considered no other than the judgement of God, especially since the Holy Spirit, dwelling in the minds of so many men of such character, brought to light the divine will.' It is clear that his contemporaries realized that so long as he lived it was hopeless to revise the creed; at any rate, no such attempt was made till after his death, much as the most prominent of the bishops disliked the formula which the Council had approved.

But the creed was to Constantine's mind of secondary importance to unity: it was intended to be the instrument whereby unity was to be achieved. It must have been not long after the Council that he issued an edict against the various minor heresites and schisms of the East, the Valentinians, the Marcionists, the Cataphrygians, the Novatians and the Paulianists – the last two had presumably not taken up the olive branch offered to them by the Council. The preamble is in terms of violent denunciation: the sects are addressed as 'enemies of the truth, foes of life and counsellors of destruction', and accused of spreading spiritual disease and eternal death by their poisonous doctrines. The operative clauses of the decree order the confiscation of their meeting-houses and prohibit them from assembling even in private houses: the Emperor expresses the hope that by attending Catholic churches they will learn the error of their ways. A supplementary constitution, published on 1 September 326, excluded the sectarians from the immunities which the Emperor had conferred on the Christian clergy. Soon afterwards Constantine had qualms about the Novatians: they were undoubtedly orthodox and pious, and might not their rigorous views be right? On 25 September the Novatians received back their churches and cemeteries.

In this edict the Emperor ignores the Arians. The heresy was officially dead, and in fact there remained very few who openly maintained it. But Constantine still remained unsatisfied, and it was his great ambition to make the unity of the Church complete and perfect by bringing within the fold the few surviving Arians and above all Arius himself. With this object, it would appear, when it was found necessary to deprive and move from Alexandria a number of priests who obstinately clung to the condemned doctrine, he deported them to Nicomedia, where they would be under his immediate supervision. The Emperor's anger is understandable when, three months later, he found that the local bishop, Eusebius, and his neighbour Theognius of Nicaea were conspiring with them against the true faith. In a characteristic outburst of rage he deprived and exiled Eusebius and Theognius, and ordered the Churches of Nicomedia and Nicaea to elect new bishops.

The Church of Nicomedia appears to have demurred to this high-handed action, and we possess the Emperor's answer. It is an extraordinary document. Opening quietly with a paraphrase of the Nicene creed, Constantine gently reproaches the Nicomedians with having deserted the true faith. And who, he asks, is the man who gave this false teaching to the innocent multitude? He proceeds to denounce Eusebius in the most intemperate terms as having been a partisan of Licinius, and as even responsible for the persecution of the Christians. He asserts that during the civil war he had sent spies against him and all but served in arms for the tyrant. These allegations, he says, he can prove by the testimony of Eusebius' priests and deacons whom he had arrested. He warns the Nicomedians that they are dangerously close to high treason in supporting Eusebius, and advises them to prove their loyalty by choosing a faithful and blameless bishop. It is not until the last paragraph that Constantine comes down to his real grievance, that Eusebius had been intriguing with the priests exiled from Alexandria. The Nicomedians and Nicaeans bowed to the storm and obediently elected new bishops, Amphion and Chrestus.

Undeterred by this rebuff, Constantine persisted in his efforts to induce Arius to submit, writing to him again and again. At length Arius overcame his not unnatural reluctance, and Constantine sent him the following invitation:

Victor Constantinus Maximus Augustus to Arius. It has long been signified to your reverence that you should come to our court, that you might enjoy our presence. We have been greatly surprised that you did not immediately do so. So now take a public vehicle and come with all speed to our court, that you may receive kindness and care from us and may be able to return to your native city. May God guard you, beloved. Dated 27 November.

Arius and one of his adherents, Euzoius, now submitted on behalf of their followers a statement of their faith, on the basis of which they petitioned for readmission to the Church. The creed which they submitted was brief and evasive, but their final request was couched in terms which were calculated to appeal to the Emperor.

Accordingly we beg your piety, God-beloved Emperor, that, since we are ecclesiastics and hold the faith and thought of the Church and of the holy scriptures, we may be united by your peace-loving and god-fearing piety to our mother the Church, all investigations and subtle arguments being set aside: that we and the Church living in peace with one another may all together make our accustomed prayers for your peaceful kingdom and all your family.

With this document in his pocket, Constantine wrote to Alexander, the bishop of Alexandria. Alexander's reply was apparently evasive and unconciliatory, and Constantine wrote again in stronger terms:

Even now will foul envy bark back with unholy sophisms of postponement? What is that to the present occasion? Do we hold other beliefs, most honoured brother, than those decided by the Holy Spirit through you all? I tell you that Arius, *the* Arius, came to me, the Augustus, on the recommendation of many persons, promising that he believed about our Catholic faith what was decided and confirmed at the Council of Nicaea by you, I your fellow-servant being present and participating in the decision. So he came to us at once with Euzoius, knowing of course the purpose of the imperial command. So I conversed with them with several others present about the word of life. I am that man who have dedicated my mind with pure faith to God. I am your fellow-servant who have undertaken all care for peace and harmony.... So I have sent to you, not merely suggesting but begging that you receive the men, who beg for pardon. If then you find that they hold firmly to the true and ever-living apostolic faith set forth at Nicæa – and they have

affirmed in our presence that this is their belief – take thought
for them all, I beg you. For if you take thought for them, you
will conquer hatred by concord. Aid concord, I beg you, offer
the blessings of friendship to those who do not doubt the faith.
Let me hear what I desire and long for, the peace and concord
of you all.

Alexander was apparently still stubborn, for Constantine
next took an important step. In the autumn of 327 he re-
assembled the Council of Nicaea.

We know nothing of the proceedings save that Arius
was readmitted to communion, and that Eusebius and
Theognius submitted a petition to the bishops. They expressed their complete submission to the sentence of the
first Council, but in order to avoid misconstruction, they
wished to make it plain they had accepted the creed, including the Homoousion, and had only objected to Arius'
excommunication on the ground that he was a misjudged
man. They were quite content to remain in exile; but now
that Arius himself had been reconciled to the Church, it
was somewhat illogical that they should remain under the
Church's ban. They therefore begged the bishops to plead
their cause with the Emperor and to review their case.
This petition was accepted, and the Emperor, having apparently forgotten his accusations of high treason, recalled
them both. Amphion and Chrestus had to stand down,
and Eusebius and Theognius were restored to Nicomedia
and Nicaea.

Constantine had to all appearances achieved his heart's
desire. The Arian schism had been finally healed and the
whole Church unanimously accepted the faith enunciated
at Nicaea; even the arch-heretic Arius himself had submitted and been reconciled to the Church. But if the Emperor hoped that his latter years would be passed in peace,
he was sorely deceived. The Origenist bishops, who had
grudgingly accepted the Nicene formula in deference to

the Emperor, watched their opponents with lynx-like eyes, and promptly seized any handle which they imprudently offered to excommunicate them: whether the charge was a doctrinal aberration or a breach of ecclesiastical discipline or even a political misdemeanour was indifferent to them. On the other hand, the Catholic party were resolved never to be reconciled with Arius, whatever his professions of faith and however many councils declared him orthodox.

Many incidents in the struggle are obscure to us. We know that during these years a considerable number of anti-Arian bishops were deposed and exiled. About the lesser fry we possess no details. In two important cases only, Marcellus of Ancyra and Eustathius of Antioch, have we further information, and this information is late and garbled. Marcellus was provoked into writing a theological treatise by the lectures of a certain Asterius, a professional rhetorician who had lapsed in the persecution and was thus precluded from his ambition of receiving an episcopal throne. His doctrines were apparently Arian in tendency, but Marcellus, whose theology was weak, went too far in combating his errors and involved himself in a dispute with both Eusebius of Nicomedia and of Caesarea, and another distinguished Origenist, Narcissus of Neronias. His doctrine was condemned at a great council held at Constantinople, attended by bishops from Thrace, Asia, Bithynia, Phrygia, Pontus and Cappadocia, and he was deposed and exiled.

Eustathius of Antioch was apparently condemned on a variety of charges. His doctrine was stated to be Sabellian: he was alleged to be the father of an illegitimate child – the mother, according to his adherents, later confessed that the father was another Eustathius, a coppersmith; and he had made some disrespectful remarks about the Emperor's mother, Helena, whose early life was, to say the

least of it, obscure; he probably disliked her as an ardent
devotee of the great Origenist scholar, Lucian of Antioch,
in whose honour she had recently built a great church at
her new city of Helenopolis.

The departure of Eustathius was the beginning of prolonged troubles at Antioch. There was a strong party which
refused to acquiesce in his deprivation or to communicate
with his successors, maintaining a schismatic Church.
Eustathius was replaced by Paulinus, bishop of Tyre, but
he died only six months later, to be followed by a certain
Eulalius. He too died soon, and on his death serious rioting broke out between the two parties. Constantine found
it necessary to employ two of his Companions, Acacius
and Strategius, to quell the disorders and to preside over
the election of the new bishop. The bishops who had assembled from the provinces of the Oriental diocese to conduct the election selected Eusebius of Caesarea; and the
people of Antioch, that is the anti-Eustathian faction, supported the proposal. Eusebius himself, however, though
naturally flattered at being offered the premier see of the
Orient, declined the perilous honour, taking shelter behind
the resolution of the Council of Nicaea, which prohibited
bishops from migrating from see to see. The question was
referred to the Emperor, whose replies to the people of
Antioch, to the assembled bishops and to Eusebius himself
are preserved. The imperial commissioners had, it would
appear, reported that the election of Eustathius' arch-
enemy to his old see would be likely to provoke disorders,
and suggested the names of two possible candidates who
would excite less contention. The Emperor therefore wrote
praising Eusebius' obedience to the laws of the Church
and recommended to the bishops George, a priest of
Arethusa, and Euphronius, a priest of the Cappadocian
Caesarea. The latter was elected, but does not seem to have
survived long: by 335 Flaccillus was bishop of Antioch.

The bishops took the opportunity of passing a number of canons. Most of them confirmed and gave greater precision to the canons of Nicaea on ecclesiastical discipline, but some are more topical. Several condemn priests who form separate communities in defiance of the bishop, and laymen who attend church but refuse to join in the prayers and in the communion but hold prayer meetings in private houses or migrate to other churches: these are evidently aimed at the supporters of Eustathius. Another canon which reveals the nervousness of the bishops provides that a newly elected bishop whom his congregation refuses to receive shall retain his see *in absentia*. But the most interesting canons are those which forbid any bishop or priest to go to court without the prior consent of the metropolitan and provincial synod, and condemn deposed bishops and priests, who, instead of appealing to a greater council, have recourse to the Emperor. It is the first sign that the ecclesiastical hierarchy was finding that a Christian emperor was not an unmixed blessing.

If we are ill-informed about the quarrels which have just been described, we have a wealth of evidence on the other great struggle of the period, the long fight between the Eusebians and Athanasius, the bishop of Alexandria, to force him to accept Arius, and eventually to unseat him. Unfortunately, the evidence is almost all from the pen of Athanasius himself, whom the later historians reproduce, and whatever view we take of that great man, no one can contend that he was a fair-minded and impartial historian. It was, in the circumstances, scarcely possible that he should be; the historical treatises that he has left us were written in the heat of the conflict and designed to prove a case, not present an impartial view. And apart from this Athanasius was a born partisan; his strength lay in his incapacity to see any point of view but his own. He cites numerous documents, it is true, but he naturally cites only those which favour his case, and he is undoubtedly guilty of serious suppressions of the truth. It never appears from his narrative, for instance, that Arius had been re-admitted to communion by a second session of the Council of Nicaea, a very material fact in the controversy, and the very fact of a second session only slips out casually when he dates his predecessor Alexander's death in April 328 as five months after the Council.

The historical controversy begins with Athanasius' own election. The only certain facts are that Alexander died on 17 April and that Athanasius was elected three weeks later, on 9 May. According to his supporters – writing over ten years later – all the laity for many days and nights besieged the church where the bishops were deliberating, cheering and shouting for Athanasius and insistently demanding his election, until at length he was duly consecrated by a majority of the bishops. His opponents tell another tale – that his election was a piece of treacherous double-dealing. The bishops according to them, had sworn to come to an agreed choice, electing no one whose qualifications were not approved by all. Many candidates were discussed, when one evening six or seven bishops, breaking their oath, clandestinely consecrated Athanasius. The rest were intimidated into acquiescence, and Athanasius wrote in the name of the Church to the Emperor, who confirmed his election.

There is probably an element of truth in both stories. The situation was delicate, for Alexander had recently admitted the Melitian bishops to communion in accordance with the decision of Nicaea: a list of them provided at his demand by Melitius is extant, and they seem to have numbered about thirty-five. Their rights during a vacancy in the chair of Alexandria, a contingency which the Nicene Council had not envisaged, were doubtful, but the Catholic bishops may have agreed for the sake of peace to elect a man acceptable to both parties. That the election was hotly contested appears from both accounts and from the dates, and there is no reason to doubt that the laity of Alexandria were strongly in favour of Athanasius. The clandestine nature of the consecration and the small number of consecrators are no doubt exaggerated, but it may well be true that an extremist group, encouraged by the cheers of the people and growing impatient of the interminable arguments with the Melitians, denounced the agreement on unanimity and proceeded to an election on their own.

The newly elected bishop of Alexandria was to prove a thorn in Constantine's side for the rest of his life. His courage and determination are indisputable; nothing would make him desert his principles. For their sake he defied all the might of the imperial government, and, even when his fellow bishops deserted him, he unflinchingly maintained that he alone was right and they were all mistaken. Constantine seems to have admired him and on occasion warmly supported him, but a clash between two such imperious personalities was inevitable. For in Athanasius' character there was none of that spirit of compromise which the Emperor's ecclesiastical policy demanded above all things. He was incapable of understanding any position but his own, and all who disagreed with him were in his eyes villains. Some scholars have seen as the dominant motive of his career an ambition to assert the authority of his see over all the churches subject to his jurisdiction. This object was certainly important in his eyes, and he was ruthless and sometimes brutal in enforcing what he considered to be ecclesiastical discipline. But even in these measures he believed that he was fighting for the truth, for he readily convinced himself that no one would oppose the lawful authority of his office unless they were intellectually and morally depraved. And in his struggle against the restoration of Arius, though he no doubt viewed with horror any reconciliation with a rebel who had stirred up the Church against his predecessor, he was fighting for the truth as he conceived it. He was perfectly right in believing that his opponents had only accepted the Nicene formula with mental reservations and that their real beliefs were unchanged. Unlike the Emperor, he preferred the truth to concord.

Constantine made his first approach to the new bishop of Alexandria on the question of Arius' restoration indirectly through Eusebius of Nicomedia. It was a tactical blunder, for Athanasius was not likely to welcome a request from the man who had originally espoused Arius' cause in defiance of Alexander. He replied defiantly to Eusebius' letter that those who had invented a heresy against the truth and had been excommunicated by the oecumenical synod (Athanasius conveniently ignores the second session) must not be received, and when Eusebius' messenger hinted at the possibility of unpleasantness with the Emperor, he complained that Eusebius was trying to intimidate him.

The Emperor then wrote himself in severe terms. We possess only the concluding sentences of his letter :

Now that you are acquainted with my will, grant unimpeded entry into the Church to all who wish it. If I hear that you have stood in the way of any of them when they claim to be members of the Church, or have debarred them entry, I will immediately send someone who will depose you at my command and remove you from the country.

It is not certain what the occasion of the threat was. Athanasius connects it with the proposed return of Arius, but it is in that case rather surprising that, though Arius was not admitted, Athanasius retained his position. It may be that Constantine wrote in sudden anger, and then changed his mind: he was very liable to such rapid fluctuations. But the letter may have concerned the Melitians, with whom Athanasius was by 330 in conflict.

In the winter of 329 or 330 Constantine received a disagreeable reminder of the Donatist controversy. He had been building a grand new church at Cirta, the capital of Numidia, to which he had given the name that it still bears, Constantine. But when the new church was completed the Donatists had forcibly taken possession of it. The Catholic bishops of Numidia wrote to the Emperor requesting that if no action was to be taken against the Donatists they might at least be granted another site, and also complaining that the Donatists had been enrolling Catholic readers and subdeacons on the city councils and imposing onerous public offices on them. We possess Constantine's reply, dated from Serdica on 5 February 330. It opens with a lengthy preamble in which the Donatists are condemned root and branch. Since it is the will of God that the human race should live in concord, it is evident that heretics and schismatics are inspired by the devil and that all their actions must of necessity be evil. After this fiery beginning, the conclusion is rather tame. The Emperor praises the Catholic bishops for their forbearance in demanding no punishment on the Donatists, 'impious criminals' though they be, 'sacrilegious and profane, faithless and irreligious, hateful to God and enemies of the Church', but rather, 'lest, in their malign and treacherous perversity, they should break into sedition and incite their like to brawls and conspiracies, and so a situation should arise which could not be pacified', leaving them to the vengeance of God. Constantine informs them that he has ordered the accountant of the diocese of Africa to make over to them another site and the consular of Numidia to erect on it another church at public expense: he has also sent to the consular an order confirming that readers and subdeacons are, like the higher clergy, immune from public duties.

After this humiliating reminder of his impotence in the face of obstinate schismatics, Constantine may well have been enraged with Athanasius on learning that his treatment of the very similar sect of the Melitians was calculated to produce an equally awkward impasse in the East, and this though the Council of Nicaea had laid down a formula for conciliation. In 331 four Melitian bishops charged Athanasius with making a forced levy of linen on the Egyptians. This charge was rebutted by two Alexandrian priests who happened to be at court representing Athanasius on some other matter. But there were apparently other accusations, for the Emperor wrote to Alexandria summoning Athanasius to court.

The next year, 332, Athanasius duly went to Nicomedia, and the charges made against him were tried before the Emperor himself in the Palace of Psammathia. He was accused of having sent a purse of gold as a bribe to one Philumenus, probably Master of the Offices, and of sacrilege. The prosecution alleged that when Athanasius was making one of his regular visitations of the Mareotes, he dispatched one of his priests named Macarius to summon before him a priest named Ischyras: Macarius burst in while Ischyras was celebrating, overturned his altar, smashed his chalice and burnt his books. Athanasius' story was that Macarius, when charged to summon Ischyras, a layman who had usurped the rank of priest, found that he was ill in bed in his own room: he accordingly instructed Ischyras' father to warn his son to desist from acting as a priest and quietly departed.

On this *cause célèbre* we can hardly hope, at this distance of time, to unravel the truth. Neither version is probably quite true. The prosecution seem to have dramatized the story by making Macarius burst in actually during mass, for the defence established that the day was not a Sunday, on which day alone it was the custom of the Egyptian Church to celebrate. On the other hand, it is difficult to believe that there was nothing in the case which Athanasius' enemies regarded as their trump card and brought up again and again, and Athanasius himself reveals at times a certain lack of confidence. He insists that Ischyras was not a genuine priest – he had, in fact, been ordained by Colluthus, the priest of Alexandria who had claimed to be a bishop in Alexander's day; that there was not and never had been any church in Ischyras' village – his church was a small dwelling-house belonging to an orphan called Ision; and as for the chalice, 'there are many cups both in private houses and in the market, and there is no sacrilege in breaking any of these; but the mystic cup, which, if it is deliberately broken, involves the perpetrator in sacrilege, is found only in the possession of lawful priests'. This is as good as admitting that Macarius did smash a cup which a bogus priest had used as a chalice in a private house which he had alleged to be a church. Athanasius' strongest card was a written confession by Ischyras himself duly signed by him and witnessed by six priests and eight deacons, that he had made the accusation under *force majeure*. It is unfortunately only too probable that this document was itself extorted by intimidation. Ischyras showed fairly clearly the value of his confession by later siding with Athanasius' accusers at the Council of Tyre.

Whatever the truth of the case, Athanasius was triumphantly acquitted at Psammathia, and the Emperor, who had evidently been impressed by his personality, sent him home with a strongly worded letter to the people of Alexandria, reproving them for their quarrels and disunion, and declaring his conviction that their bishop was a man of God. The Melitians, however, were not discouraged, but endeavoured to reopen the charge of the broken chalice, and at the same time brought forward a still more serious accusation, that Athanasius had murdered the Melitian bishop of Hypsele, Arsenius: a severed human hand was produced which, it was alleged, was all that was left of the corpse. Constantine refused to reopen the chalice case, which he had already tried, and ordered his half-brother, Delmatius, the censor, to try the murder charge at Antioch. Athanasius disproved the accusation in the most convincing manner possible, by proving that his alleged victim was alive.

On this second *cause célèbre* the evidence is even more tangled than on the first. Athanasius later represented that the case was deliberately framed against him by John Arcaph, Melitius' successor as head of the 'Church of the Martyrs'. This is probably a libel, for not only was Athanasius – not a forgiving character – reconciled with John after the case collapsed, but Constantine invited John to the palace in the most flattering terms. Arsenius had undoubtedly been missing for five or six years, and according to the Melitians the last thing known of him was that Plusianus, one of Athanasius' bishops, had lashed him to a post in his own house and flogged him, and then locked the room and set the house on fire. He had escaped through the window, but on his subsequent disappearance his colleagues had naturally suspected foul play. He had, in fact, it appeared later, found refuge in a little monastery in the neighbouring countryside, whence he escaped to Tyre. Athanasius never denies this lurid story, and it may be substantially true.

However this may be, Constantine was furious on learning that the Melitians had made a fool of him, cancelled the trial, and wrote a long letter to Athanasius, which he requested him to read frequently in public, denouncing 'the perverse and lawless Melitians' for their malicious calumnies, both in the matter of the alleged broken chalice and the alleged murder of Arsenius, and threatening that if they did any such thing again he would himself try them under the civil law, and no longer under the law of the Church.

It was apparently about this time that Arius, who had now waited six years since his readmission to communion by the second session of Nicaea and was still debarred by Athanasius from returning to Alexandria, sent a petition to Constantine. Its drift can be discerned from some sentences from it which Constantine quotes in reply: 'Either let us have that of which we have already been granted possession, or let it be done as we ourselves wish.' 'We are being driven out, and are being deprived of our right to be received back.' 'What shall we do then, if no one thinks fit to receive us?' Arius also claimed that all the people of Libya were on his side. From other passages it appears that he submitted another doctrinal statement, in which he raised subtle distinctions about essence and substance.

Arius may have been hoping that Athanasius' intransigent attitude would induce the Emperor to look favourably on his proposition, which seems to have been that since Athanasius, defying the decision of the oecumenical council, refused to reinstate him in Alexandria, he should be allowed to return to Libya, where he had much popular support, together with his followers, who included Secundus of Ptolemais, the metropolitan of the province. If so, Arius was gravely disappointed. His petition infuriated Constantine, as being in the first place a covert attack on the faith of Nicaea, and in the second place as proposing the erection of a schismatic church in Libya. His reply was an open letter to Arius and the Arians, in which he denounced Arius' heretical views and schismatical proposals in the most violent and abusive terms. This letter was by his orders read in the presence of Paterius, the

Prefect of Egypt, in his palace at Alexandria. The same official messengers who brought this letter also carried an edict addressed to all the bishops and their flocks, ordering that all the works of Arius should be publicly burned, that anyone in whose possession they were subsequently found should be liable to the death penalty, and that henceforth his supporters should be called Porphyrians, since Arius was as great an enemy of the Christian faith as that notorious protagonist of paganism.

These extraordinary outbursts show that Constantine was losing all control of his temper. Baffled and infuriated by the open defiance and the covert intrigues which from every side frustrated his plain and simple demand for concord on the basis of the decisions of the oecumenical council, he struck out now at one side and now at the other, according as the one irritated him or the other secured his ear. He was now beginning to feel that time was growing short. For he was planning to celebrate his thirtieth anniversary with a second great council, which should mark the completion of his task of unifying the Church, initiated by the first great council held on his twentieth anniversary. He had long been building a magnificent church on the site of the Holy Sepulchre of Jerusalem, and it was his plan that, every quarrel having been resolved, all the bishops of the Church should meet to dedicate it. The Tricennalia would fall in 335, and in the spring of 334 Constantine ordered the convocation of a council at Caesarea under the presidency of Eusebius 'for the purification of the holy Christian people'.

The choice of president shows that Constantine had by this time come under the influence of the group of bishops, headed by Eusebius, who were working for Arius' restoration and regarded Athanasius as the chief obstacle to their designs. Community of interest had naturally drawn together Athanasius' Melitian victims and Arius' friends. The former looked for patrons, who would gain the Emperor's ear for their complaints, and the bishop of Nicomedia, where Constantine often resided, would be a very useful friend to them. On the other hand, the two Eusebii, looking for a lever whereby to force Athanasius to receive Arius back to Alexandria, found the Melitians convenient tools. Athanasius represents the attacks on him as being from the very beginning a conspiracy encouraged by his chief enemy, Eusebius of Nicomedia, and promptly dubbed the Melitians Arians. But this is a prejudiced view, which disregards the fact that the Melitians had very real grievances of their own. How early the alliance sprang up we do not know, but the first open step was this Council of Caesarea.

. Although the summons to the Council went out in the Emperor's name, Athanasius refused to attend, alleging that the court before which he was to be tried was composed of his enemies. Constantine must have accepted this excuse, for it was not till over a year later, on the very eve of the Tricennalia, that, having changed his mind again, he ordered the convocation of a second council, this time at Tyre. In his letter to the Council, Constantine makes a strong appeal for unity and concord, and bitterly denounces those who, inflamed by a spirit of contention, are endeavouring to throw the whole Church into confusion. He announces that he has summoned those bishops whom the Council wished to attend and take part in the proceedings, and that he is also sending a high official, the Companion and consular Dionysius, to supervise the proceedings and in particular to maintain order, and also to remind those who ought to attend:

For if anyone, which I think unlikely, should even now try to defy our command and refuse to attend the synod, we shall dispatch from here one who will by imperial order expel him and teach him that he never ought to have resisted the decrees of the Emperor which were issued on behalf of the truth.

The allusion to Athanasius' contumacy in the previous year is unmistakable. He ends by urging the Council to judge impartially, unbiased by hostility or favour, 'that you may free the Church from all blasphemy and lighten my cares, and by restoring the grace of peace to those who are at strife may afford yourselves the greatest happiness'.

Athanasius, after long hesitation, eventually yielded to the menacing summons of the Emperor. 'Athanasius is very despondent,' as we learn from a contemporary letter which chance has preserved from the rubbish-heaps of Egypt. 'They have often come to fetch him and so far he has not started. He put his luggage aboard as if he were starting, and again he took the luggage off the ship a second time, not wishing to start.' He had reason to be despondent, for though he took with him forty-eight loyal Egyptian bishops, the Council had been packed with many of his open enemies. And, it must be admitted, the charges against him were formidable and many of them well-founded.

Proceedings started with the imperial commissioner, Dionysius, in the chair, supported by lay officers of the court and ushers: Athanasius' partisans were later to claim that this vitiated the ecclesiastical character of the Council, but they do not seem to have complained at the time. Athanasius entered a protest against the presence of many personal enemies on the Council which was to try him, but his objection was overruled: it does not seem, in fact, to have been valid in the light of the general practice of the Church. The hearing of the charges then began.

Athanasius, in his account to the Council, gives the impression that there was one charge only, the old case of Macarius and the broken chalice. But we have from another source a summary of the official minutes of the Council, which show that there were many others. Ischyras complained not only of the breaking of the chalice, but that Athanasius had imprisoned him and falsely charged him before Hyginus, the prefect of Egypt, with having stoned the statue of the Emperor, and so got him into gaol. Callinicus, the Melitian bishop of Pelusium, who had been reconciled with Alexander, complained that he had been deposed because he refused to communicate with Athanasius until he had cleared himself of the chalice charge, and had then been subjected to trial, torture and imprisonment by the military authorities. Five other Melitian bishops complained of having been flogged. With regard to Arsenius, the accusers admitted their error, but claimed that their suspicion had been justified by the brutal treatment which Athanasius' supporters had inflicted upon him and the mysterious manner in which he had disappeared. Finally, the validity of Athanasius' election was challenged: the story of his clandestine ordination in violation of the oath of assembled bishops was brought up, and the official record of some meeting was read, in which the populace shouted that they refused because of Athanasius to come to church.

Athanasius never mentions any of the accusations of violence. This fact in itself gives rise to suspicion, and this suspicion is reinforced by the contemporary letter cited above, which was written by a Melitian, it is true, but reads like a straightforward, if biased, report of the news of the town. The writer depicts Athanasius' followers, acting in concert with the troops under the command of the military governor of Alexandria, beating up any Melitians they could lay hands on 'and making them all bloody, so that their life was in danger', intimidating and knocking about the one innkeeper who still dared to take in Melitian visitors, and arresting and imprisoning Melitian bishops, priests and deacons. Athanasius evidently had the military authorities in his pocket and did not scruple to invoke their aid.

But if there were a number of valid charges against Athanasius, the Council does not seem to have handled them in an impartial spirit. This appears particularly from the case of the broken chalice, on which Athanasius gives a wealth of documentation. Some of his objections are, it is true, groundless. He protests because the accused, Macarius, had been arrested and was kept in chains; but the author of the letter cited above suggests that this had been done at the Emperor's orders, because some emissaries of Athanasius had endeavoured to spirit him away before the Council. When it was decided to send a subcommission of the Council to investigate on the spot, Athanasius objected that the investigation was superfluous, as the facts were already established; but this was begging the question. When, however, it came to the selection of the members of the subcommission, the bias of the Council became evident, for six bishops were chosen who were well known as supporters of Arius and enemies of Athanasius. Formal protests were addressed by the forty-eight Egyptian bishops of Athanasius' party to the Council and to the imperial commissioner, and Alexander, bishop of Thessalonica, also wrote to the latter. The commissioner was impressed by this last complaint and wrote to the leaders of the anti-Athanasian group, reminding them of his previous instructions to choose the commissioners by an agreed resolution, and warning them that they were giving a handle to those who wished to criticize the conduct of the Council. He allowed himself to be over-persuaded, however, and the commission, as already constituted, went to work.

Its proceedings are known to us from a long series of protests, addressed by the priests and deacons of Alexandria and of Mareotes to the Council, the commission, the Prefect of Egypt and sundry other officials, objecting that neither the accused, Macarius, nor Athanasius, nor they themselves were allowed to be present. It is clear that the commission was determined to hear only one side of the case. Further allegations by Athanasius that the witnesses were suborned, and that intimidation was used to extract their evidence, and that their evidence none the less failed to substantiate all the accusations, probably have a good deal of truth in them. The brief extracts quoted by Athanasius from the official minutes seem to prove that Ischyras was ill in bed in his room when Macarius paid his visit and that his accusation that Macarius had burnt his service books was false. Witnesses were, however, found to testify that they were in the church when Macarius came in and upset the holy table.

On the failure of their first protest the Egyptian bishops present at the Council wrote again to Dionysius, the imperial commissioner, asking him to reserve the decision of the case for the Emperor. Dionysius very properly ignored this uncanonical appeal, and Athanasius and the Egyptian delegation withdrew from the Council. The Council proceeded to condemn Athanasius *in absentia*, deprive him of his bishopric, and inhibit him from residing at Alexandria. They next received into communion and reinstated the Melitian clergy. Finally, they reported their proceedings to the Emperor and to all bishops, reciting the whole history of the case from Athanasius' contumacious refusal to attend the Council of Caesarea in defiance of the Emperor's summons to his final withdrawal, and commenting severely on his insolent and disorderly behaviour during the Council, where he abused and insulted his colleagues and refused to answer many charges.

An imperial notary, Marianus, now arrived and delivered to the Council an invitation from the Emperor to attend the dedication of the great church of the Holy Sepulchre, commanding them first to resolve all quarrels among themselves, that with hearts purified of discord they might celebrate the feast in a proper spirit. Eusebius gives a lyrical account of the assembly, which was, he says, the greatest that he had seen, and included bishops from every province, Palestine, Arabia, Phoenicia, Syria, Mesopotamia and Cilicia in the Orient; Egypt, Libya and the Thebaid – presumably represented by the Melitians; Cappadocia and Bithynia in Asia Minor; Thrace, Macedonia, Moesia and Pannonia in Europe, and even Persians from beyond the bounds of the Empire. For the bishops magnificent banquets were prepared, while vast quantities of food, clothes and money were distributed to the poor. The bishops in response 'adorned the feast with prayers and sermons, some hymning the devotion to the Saviour of all of the God-beloved Emperor, and describing his mighty works about the basilica, and others providing for all to hear a banquet of spiritual nourishment in displays of theological learning'. Others not so gifted gave expositions of the holy scriptures, and the rank and file celebrated the occasion by performing liturgies and praying 'on behalf of the general peace, the Church of God and the Emperor himself, the cause of these good things, and his God-beloved sons'.

One thing only remained to crown the Emperor's design, and this the Council accomplished. A letter arrived from Constantine stating that he had received from Arius and his followers an orthodox confession of faith, which he had personally and *viva voce* examined and accepted; he accordingly urged the bishops to approve the confession, which was enclosed, and receive the authors into communion. The Council gratefully acceded to this request, and wrote a fulsome letter to the Churches of Alexandria, Egypt, Libya and the Thebaid, expressing their confidence that the recipients would rejoice in being reunited to their brothers and fathers, the limbs of their own body. Constantine's great desire seemed at last to be fulfilled: the whole Church – if one could conveniently forget the still rebellious Donatists in Africa and the Novatians – was united in brotherly love.

It must have been during the celebrations at Jerusalem that Athanasius decided on a personal appeal to the Emperor, before he should receive the report of the Council. He arrived at Constantinople on 30 October, attended by only four bishops. Constantine himself describes their meeting:

As I was entering Constantinople, the fortunate city which bears our name, from a suburban palace, he advanced into the middle of the road with some others that he had with him, mourning and lamenting, and so sudden was his advance as to give us cause for astonishment. For God who sees all bears witness that I was unable at first sight to recognize who he was, had not some of our servants explained on our inquiry who he was and what injustice he had suffered from you. So troubled and downcast did we see the man that we felt unspeakable pity for him, knowing him to be that Athanasius, the holy sight of whom was sufficient to draw even the Gentiles to reverence the God of all.

Under the influence of the dominating personality of Athanasius, the Emperor immediately changed his mind. It is not very clear what Constantine had expected of the Council of Tyre; perhaps he had wishfully hoped for reconciliation. But, however that may be, on the unsupported evidence of one of the interested parties, he condemned the whole proceedings in no uncertain terms. 'I do not know,' he wrote to the bishops who had attended the synod,

what was decided by your council with such tempestuous tumult, but it appears that the truth has been somehow distorted by violent disorder, since, owing to your contentiousness towards your neighbours, which you desire to be invincible, you do not observe what is pleasing to God. But let it be the work of the divine providence manifestly to convict and dis-

sipate the horrid deeds of your quarrelsomeness, or rather fight
for evil, and to demonstrate to you clearly whether you had
any care for the truth when you assembled at Tyre and whether
the judgements which you made were free from any favour or
enmity. I therefore wish you all to come without delay to my
Prudence in order that you may personally in my presence give
an accurate account of what you have done.

But the Council of Tyre was not to reassemble and
account to the Emperor for its findings. A few days later a
number of bishops who had attended the Council, including
the two Eusebii, arrived at Constantinople to join in the
celebration of the Tricennalia. Under their influence
Constantine changed his mind once more. We have only
Athanasius' account of what happened, and according to
him they brought a new charge against him, that he had
threatened to prevent the shipment of the corn which was
sent from Alexandria to feed Constantinople. Athanasius objected that, as a poor man without any official status, he
could not have made any such threat, but Eusebius retorted that he was rich and powerful and capable of anything. Eusebius' estimate of Athanasius' position was
nearer to the truth than his own; but one may doubt if
Constantine would have been greatly impressed by the
alleged threat apart from its context, and Athanasius char-
acteristically does not tell us why he was alleged to have
made it. It may be suspected that he was accused of having
declared that if the Emperor forced him to take back the
Arians and Melitians, he would retaliate by stopping the
shipment of corn from Alexandria, and the story may have
convinced Constantine of Athanasius' intransigence. At
all events the Emperor promptly exiled Athanasius to
Trèves in Gaul, and he left Constantinople on 7 November,
exactly a week after he had arrived.

This extraordinary series of contradictory decisions
shows that Constantine's temper had by now grown very

short. The obstinate refusal of the bishops to obey his simple behest to live in peace and unity was doubly irritating to him. As emperor he was used to being obeyed, but still more did he expect the bishops to pay due respect to his position as 'the true servant of God, which not even you would deny'. He bitterly complains in his letter recalling the Council of Tyre that

now even the barbarians, because of me, the true servant of God, have recognized God and learnt to respect Him, Who, they have learned by experience, everywhere protects me and takes thought for me. They respect Him because of their fear of me, but we [Constantine speaks as a member of the Church, almost a bishop] who are supposed to protect – I would not say preserve – the sacred mysteries of His favour – we, I say, do nothing but what tends to strife and hatred, and to speak plainly, the destruction of the human race.

At the great Council of Jerusalem he had hoped at last to see his dream of a united Church fulfilled, and before he received the report of the Council of Tyre he seems to have imagined that unanimity had been actually achieved. Then he had learned that Athanasius had been expelled from the Church, and had for a brief moment believed that he was a deeply wronged man, the victim of a hostile cabal. Then, hearing the other side, he had seen in Athanasius the chief obstacle to unity. He was baffled and he banished the protagonists of both sides, Athanasius and John Arcaph, the Melitian leader. But he still hoped. Though he exiled Athanasius, he refused to accept his deprivation or to allow another bishop to be elected in his place: he might yet see the light.

When Arius and his associates, returning to Egypt in accordance with the decision of the Council of Jerusalem, were refused communion by the Egyptian bishops, Constantine, rather than start fresh brawls, recalled them to Constantinople to await happier times. Arius did not long survive his recall. Athanasius relates with unction the final judgement of God on his enemy. The Eusebian party were resolved that, despite his rebuff in Egypt, Arius should receive official recognition as a loyal member of the Church. They therefore persuaded the Emperor to order Alexander, bishop of Constantinople, despite his bitter protests, to allow him to communicate in the cathedral of the capital city. But on the Saturday before the Sunday fixed for the great event, Arius, on his way from the palace, felt the call of nature and took refuge in a public convenience. His companions waited, but he did not reappear. At length they broke in and found him dead upon the seat.

Constantine was to die a disappointed man. During the eighteen months that he was still to live after the Council of Jerusalem, the quarrels of the Church remained unresolved. Athanasius remained obdurate and was not recalled. The Egyptian clergy remained loyal to him and refused to admit the Arians, or, it would seem, the Melitians. In the West the Donatists persisted in their defiance: at the very end of the reign they addressed Gregory, the praetorian prefect of Africa, as a 'blot on the senate and disgrace to the prefects'. Constantine little knew how hard a task he had taken upon himself when he assumed the duty as God's servant of bringing concord to His Church.

13 Bishop of Those Outside the Church

Constantine once remarked to an assembly of bishops whom he was entertaining: 'You are the bishops of those within the Church, but I would be a bishop established by God of those outside it.' These words are an understatement of what Constantine conceived to be his position. Both his words and his actions demonstrate that he regarded himself responsible before God for the inner well-being of the Church, and especially for its unity. But towards his pagan subjects he felt that God, in giving him the sovereign power, had laid upon him a special responsibility.

It was naturally his own subjects for whom he felt himself chiefly answerable. He does not seem to have promoted missionary work beyond the bounds of the empire, and he considered that the best form of propaganda among the barbarians was to demonstrate by military victories the power of the Mighty One who had caused him to prevail over all his enemies. During the last decade of his reign he had an opportunity of doing this. In 331 the Goths broke through the Danube frontier, but the Roman armies, led by the Caesar Constantine, the Emperor's eldest surviving son, soundly defeated them in the following year and chased them back across the frontier. Two years later the Sarmatians, defeated by the Goths and faced by a rebellion of their own subject tribes, paid Constantine the compliment of begging to be received within the Empire.

Large numbers of the able-bodied men were enrolled in the imperial armies, and the remainder were planted as agricultural colonists in Italy and in the devastated Balkan provinces, Macedonia, Thrace and Scythia. These successes no doubt impressed upon the Goths the power of Christianity, which had been introduced among them two gen-generations earlier by Roman prisoners, but had hitherto made little progress: a few years after Constantine's death they were converted by the missionary efforts of Ulfilas, an emissary of the Gothic king at Constantinople, instructed by Eusebius, who had by then been translated from Nicomedia to the new capital.

On the eastern frontier the little kingdom of Iberia officially adopted the Christian faith during Constantine's reign. We possess the story of the conversion only in a late and legendary form. A Christian woman, carried off into captivity from the Roman Empire into Iberia, excited notice by her ascetic life, and was called in as a last resort by the queen of the country to cure her ailing son. The son recovered and the queen was converted. The king, lost in a fog while out hunting, asked aid of the God whose powers his wife had tested with success, and the fog cleared. He too accepted the new faith and sent an emissary to Constantine to ask for instructors to teach his subjects. Though the details of the story are unreliable, there is no doubt that it was at this date that the ancient Church of Iberia, or as it is today known, Georgia, was founded.

Another rather similar story is told of the conversion of the kingdom of Axum, the ancestor of the modern Ethiopia, but here the story is both more credible and better attested. A Tyrian philosopher named Meropius made a voyage to India, taking with him two boys, Aedesius and Frumentius, who were related to him and whom he was educating. On the return voyage their ship put in for water and supplies on the Axumite coast, unaware that the treaty between Axum and Rome which guaranteed protection to Roman subjects had expired. The ship was boarded by the natives and all its occupants put to the sword except the two boys, who were sent as presents to the king. He found their talents useful, and eventually promoted Aedesius to be his cup-bearer and Frumentius to be his treasurer and secretary. On his death the king manumitted the brothers, but on the urgent request of the queen they continued to hold office during the minority of her son Aeizanas. Frumentius was now virtually regent of the Axumite kingdom, and he used his position to encourage Christian merchants from the Roman Empire to settle and build churches and propagate the faith. On Aeizanas' attaining his majority the brothers received permission to return home, and Aedesius never returned, becoming a priest in his native city of Tyre: it was from him that the Church historian Rufinus obtained the story. Frumentius went to Athanasius at Alexandria and asked him to follow up his missionary efforts by consecrating a bishop for Axum. Athanasius not unnaturally selected Frumentius himself for the post, and he returned to spend the rest of his life at Axum. His efforts were eventually crowned by the conversion of Aeizanas himself, as his later coins and inscriptions attest.

In the Persian Empire Christianity had long been established in the areas adjacent to the Roman dominions; a bishop from Persia had attended the Council of Nicaea. On their behalf Constantine intervened diplomatically, when soon after the fall of Licinius the Persian king Sapor negotiated with him for a treaty of alliance. Constantine's letter to Sapor, which Eusebius has preserved in a Greek translation, is a very curious document, but there is no serious reason to doubt its authenticity. The Emperor as usual justifies his belief in the God of the Christians by his own victorious career:

With the power of this God as my ally, starting from the bounds of Ocean, I have raised up all the world to firm hopes of salvation, so that all the regions which, enslaved by so many tyrants and yielding to their daily calamities, had been utterly ruined, have on being recovered for the commonwealth revived as under a physician's care. This God, I reverence, Whose symbol my army, an army dedicated to God, bears upon its shoulders.

He goes on to recall the disasters which had befallen the emperors who had persecuted the Christian faith, picking out for special mention Valerian, who had died a prisoner of the Persians. At the same time he emphasizes that the Christian God enjoins peace, humility and loyalty on His followers, and abhors violence and pride and sedition. Finally, he urges Sapor to be gracious to his Christian subjects and thus to win the favour of the Lord of all.

This letter probably did more harm than good. Christians had hitherto enjoyed toleration in the Persian Empire, but henceforth they were more than ever suspect, not only as traitors to the national religion, Zoroastrianism, but as protégés and possible agents of the national enemy. For several years fear of Constantine's military power induced Sapor both to keep the peace and to tolerate the Christians, but shortly before Constantine's death he opened hostilities and within a few years began to persecute.

The Armenian kingdom was already Christian when Constantine conquered the East. King Tiridates, after being expelled by the Persians in his boyhood and spending his youth as a refugee at the Roman court (where he may well have met young Constantine), was restored to his kingdom in 297 as a result of Galerius' victory over the Persians. He was at this time still a pagan, and even copied his patron Diocletian in instituting in 303 a persecution of Christians in Armenia, where missionary work had begun over a generation before. Before 312, however, he

had been converted by Gregory 'the illuminator', and
proceeded to suppress paganism with equal zeal, destroying the temples and confiscating their estates to endow the
new faith. He thus fell foul of Maximin, who in 312 invaded his kingdom without success. Friendly relations
were re-established with the Empire on the fall of Maximin
in the following year, and Constantine signed a treaty of
alliance with him: according to the Armenian historians
Tiridates personally travelled with Gregory to Rome or
Dalmatia (Armenian geography of the west is vague) to
meet the Christian emperor. Tiridates was succeeded by
his son Chosroes and he by his son Tigranes, both of
whom pursued Tiridates' pro-Christian and pro-Roman
policy. About 334 Tigranes was treacherously kidnapped
and blinded by a neighbouring Persian satrap and a Persian
army occupied the country. The Armenian nobility naturally appealed to Constantine, offering him the kingdom,
and Constantine promptly took up the offer, appointing
his nephew Hannibalianus 'King of kings': he was preparing for a Persian war when death overtook him. In
Armenia Constantine's zeal for Christianity thus fell into
line with the traditional Roman policy of supporting a
national dynasty or establishing a Roman client king in
Armenia in opposition to the Persian claim to suzerainty.

In dealing with his own subjects, Constantine had per-
force to move slowly. The vast majority of them were still
pagan, and among the upper classes, from whom he had
to draw most of his officials, Christians were particularly
rare. Most important of all, the army, despite Constantine's propaganda, was still mainly pagan: we possess an
official record of the acclamations with which the Emperor was greeted by his victorious army shortly after
the defeat of Licinius, and it runs: 'Constantine Augustus,
may the gods preserve you! Your safety is our safety! We
speak the truth! We speak under oath!' In these circum-

stances Constantine could not with safety take very drastic measures against paganism, but we can observe him, during the last twelve years of his reign, when he held sole power, gaining in confidence and losing patience with the obstinate blindness of his subjects.

When he first conquered Licinius, rumours had apparently gone round that pagan worship was to be banned. These rumours Constantine denied in an edict, the greater part of which is devoted to propaganda for Christianity. He recalls the great persecution which he himself had witnessed, and points to the exemplary fate of the persecutors. He attributes his own triumph to God: 'And this I pray not without reason, O Lord of all, holy God: for under Thy leadership I set on foot and accomplished deeds of salvation, and displaying Thy symbol everywhere I led my army to victory.' He prays to God to grant peace to all his subjects without distinction; but he makes it plain that the pagans little deserve it: 'Let those who err gladly enjoy the same peace and tranquillity as those who believe. For this sweetness of fellowship will have power to raise them up also, and to lead them on to the right path.' He warns the Christians against intolerance, but he grants toleration to the pagans in contemptuous language. 'Let no one annoy his neighbour; let each have and enjoy what his soul desires. Those who are wise must be sure that they alone will live a pure and holy life whom Thou callest to rest in Thy holy laws. But let those who hold aloof possess if they wish the temples of falsehood; we possess the glorious house of Thy truth.' In a final paragraph Constantine again insists on toleration for the pagans: 'For it is one thing to undertake of one's free will the struggle for immortality, but another to enforce it with penalties.' He denies that pagan worship – the customs of the temples and power of darkness – has been prohibited, 'though I would have given this advice to all men, were not the

violent resistance of wicked error rooted in the souls of
some to the detriment of our common salvation.'

After this the pagans can have entertained no doubts of
Constantine's wishes, and must have felt a little insecure in
the grudging and contemptuous toleration offered to them.
How far Constantine went in a direct attack on pagan
worship it is difficult, owing to the tendentiousness of our
records, to determine. He certainly suppressed a few famous temples, that of Asclepius at Aegae of Cilicia, famed
for its miraculous cures, and those of Apheca and Heliopolis in Phoenicia : these were centres of ritual prostitution
and therefore particularly repugnant to Christian senti-
ment.

It is also certain that Constantine carried out a thorough
spoliation of the temples. Many of their famous works of
art were carried off to decorate his new capital, and many
had to surrender their bronze doors, and even their bronze
roof tiles. At a later date two commissioners were appointed who toured the provinces, systematically confiscating
all gold objects in the temples, stripping even the cult images of their gold plating and returning only their wooden
cores. Eusebius represents their proceedings as primarily
religious moves, designed to throw ridicule on the idols
which pagans worshipped. It seems more likely that Constantine's motive was mainly fiscal, though he no doubt
welcomed the opportunity to lower the prestige of the pagan
gods. It is possible also that Constantine confiscated the
lands of the temples, once more mainly for fiscal reasons.

But when Eusebius declares that shortly after his victory over Licinius Constantine prohibited 'the vile rites
of idolatry which were practised of old in town and country, so that no one should dare to erect images, or to attempt divination and other vanities, or sacrifice at all,' he
is obviously exaggerating, for the edict cited above makes
it plain that pagans were allowed to practise their religion

in their temples. In all probability the Emperor promulgated in the East his previous regulations against divination and private sacrifices, and it was this that provoked the exaggerated rumours which he contradicted in his edict. In the light of this, Eusebius' later statement that Constantine in a number of constitutions issued general prohibitions against 'sacrificing to idols, practising divination, erecting images, and performing secret initiations', is suspect. Yet it may well be true that in his latter years Constantine took the final step of prohibiting even public sacrifices. No such constitution survives in the Code, but a law issued in 341 by his son Constantius orders that 'superstition shall cease and the madness of sacrifices shall be abolished,' and lays down penalties for 'whoever contrary to the law of the late Emperor, my father, and this my command dares to celebrate sacrifices'. The frequent iteration of this prohibition for the next half-century proves that it was not and could not be enforced.

The imperial cult caused but little embarrassment to Constantine. Though he could hardly countenance his own worship, he had no wish to suppress an institution which gave to the provincials their sole means of expressing their loyalty to the Emperor, and which incidentally provided the populace with games and festivals and the leading provincial families with titles of honour. The imperial cult had in fact become a social institution of admitted value. The provincial councils which celebrated it were a useful check on the governors and officials, since they possessed sufficient independence to complain effectively of their misconduct. The provincial high priests, whom the councils annually elected, had to pay for the honour by providing games at their own expense or subscribing for the erection of public buildings, but the post was valued, partly for the prestige which it carried and partly for the immunities which it earned, and provided a suitable reward for wealthy and public-spirited town councillors. Moreover, the cult had become so secularized that it gave little offence to Christians. A council of Spanish bishops, probably held shortly before the great persecution, had implicitly permitted Christians to hold provincial priesthoods, provided that they did not sacrifice, by prescribing penances for those who only celebrated games.

Constantine therefore contented himself with suppressing the actual cult, prohibiting the erection of his statue in any pagan temple. An inscription from Hispellum in Umbria, dating from the last years of his reign, reveals his attitude. The cities of Umbria had hitherto been grouped with those of Tuscia for the purpose of the cult, and they now asked leave to build a temple of their own to the imperial house and to hold theatrical and gladiatorial shows under their own high priest. Constantine granted all their requests, only specifying that 'the temple dedicated to our name shall not be polluted with the falsehoods of any contagious superstition'.

At the same time that he was despoiling the temples of their artistic treasures and robbing them of their endowments, Constantine lavished public money on building magnificent churches and providing the Christian communities with a regular income. He made to all churches annual allocations of corn which the bishops distributed to the clergy and to the poor, and, directly after the defeat of Licinius, he made public funds available for the repair and enlargement of existing churches and the erection of new churches where needed. Eusebius has preserved his copy of the circular letter which the Emperor addressed to all metropolitans of provinces announcing this measure:

Victor Constantinus Maximus Augustus to Eusebius. Seeing that up to the present time the unholy will of the tyrant has persecuted the servants of the Saviour God, I believe and have convinced myself that the fabric of all churches is either decayed through neglect or is, through fear of impending injury, inferior to what it should be, dearest brother. Now that freedom has been restored, and that serpent has been expelled from the administration of the commonwealth by the providence of the Greatest God and by my agency, I think that the divine power has been made manifest to all, and that those who through fear or lack of faith fell into sin will recognize the Truly Existent One and will return to the true and right way of life. Accordingly you are to take active measures about the fabric of all churches over which you preside or over which you know other bishops of the area or priests or deacons to preside, either repairing those that exist or enlarging them or where need demands building new churches. You, and the others through you, will demand what is required from the provincial governors and the office of praetorian prefects: they have been instructed to carry out your holiness's orders with all dispatch. God will preserve you, beloved brother.

In the more important cities Constantine built churches of especial splendour. Eusebius picks out for special mention the cathedral of the imperial residence, Nicodemia, and the great Golden Church of Antioch, which was not completed till several years after the Emperor's death. Constantine's own city was naturally equipped with a set of magnificent basilicas, of which those dedicated to the Holy Apostles, the Holy Wisdom and the Holy Peace are the most famous. Nor did the Emperor neglect the West. In Rome he added two new basilicas, those of St Peter and of St Paul, to his previous benefactions, endowing them with extensive landed estates in the eastern provinces, which brought in an annual revenue of 3,710 and 4,070 *solidi* respectively: the bulk of the rents came in both cases from Egypt, but St Peter's was appropriately given some lands in Antioch and St Paul's some in Tarsus. Lesser cities of the West also continued to enjoy Constantine's munificence: we have seen that at Cirta, the capital of Numidia, a basilica was completed at the Emperor's expense in 329, and that when it was seized by the Donatists, another was promptly begun.

It was, however, on the Holy Land that Constantine concentrated his efforts. At Jerusalem excavations were conducted on the supposed site of the Holy Sepulchre, and after the demolition of a temple of Aphrodite and the removal of a great mound on which it stood, a cave was discovered which was identified with the tomb. Eusebius has preserved the letter which Constantine wrote to Macarius, bishop of Jerusalem, on receiving this tremendous news. He declares his desire that not only shall a basilica be erected finer than any other in the world, but that the new buildings shall surpass the most magnificent monuments that any city possesses. He informs Macarius that he has already instructed the governor of the province and Dracialianus, the deputy of the praetorian prefects in the diocese of the Orient, to provide craftsmen, labourers, and materials in whatever quantities he may demand, and he invites the bishop to specify what columns and marbles he requires from other parts of the empire, and to consider the question of the roof, suggesting that a gilded coffered ceiling would be provided if the bishop so desired. The vast complex of buildings, which comprised, in addition to the rotunda over the actual tomb and the great basilica, a spacious paved court surrounded by colonnades, took nearly ten years to build.

Constantine's aged mother, Helena Augusta, paid a visit to the Holy Land in her last years, and celebrated the occasion by building two other great churches, one over the cave of the nativity at Bethlehem, and the other on the Mount of Olives on the place of the Ascension. Another lady of the imperial family, Eutropia, the mother of Fausta, later visited Palestine, and reported to her son-in-law that Mamre (Hebron), the hallowed spot where Abraham had entertained – according to the Christian interpretation of the incident – the Son of God with two angels, was now a pagan sanctuary. Constantine wrote in sharp reproof to Macarius and the other bishop of Palestine, asking them why they had tolerated this sacrilege, and informing them that he had instructed Acacius, the imperial Companion then in charge of the diocese of the Orient, to destroy the altars and remove the idols, and to build a basilica on the site 'worthy of the Catholic and Apostolic Church'.

Constantine added little to the legal privileges of the Church during the latter part of his reign. One, indeed, the immunity of the clergy from service on town councils, he had to restrict. The effect of the grant had been that there had been a rush of well-to-do persons into holy orders, and the problem, already serious, of finding a sufficient number of candidates to fill vacancies had been seriously aggravated. In a somewhat acid constitution dated 326, Constantine laid down that for the future clergy were not to be ordained recklessly and without regard to the size of a city, but only to supply vacancies caused by death, and that persons who were of the families of town councillors or possessed the requisite property qualification to be enrolled should be debarred from holy orders: 'For the wealthy ought to support the requirements of this world, and the poor be maintained by the riches of the Church.'

One extraordinary extension made to the powers of the bishop shows, however, how far Constantine had travelled in his devotion to the Church. In a constitution dated 333 he gently rebukes his praetorian prefect Ablabius, who, though a zealous Christian, had doubted whether he had interpreted the Emperor's will rightly, for questioning the rule that either party in a civil suit could, despite the other's objection, demand the jurisdiction of the local bishop, and the bishop's verdict should be final and inappellable and should be executed by the civil authority. This ruling was revoked after Constantine's death, and bishops later retained only a voluntary jurisdiction with the consent of both parties.

By all these measures Constantine worked to increase the prestige and splendour of the Christian Church, to impoverish and bring into contempt the temples of the pagan gods, and finally, it may be, to abolish the pagan cult. Positive propaganda for the Christian faith he left to the Church except in the army and the court. His measures to christianize the army, which began before his last struggle with Licinius, have been already described. His personal efforts to convert his court appear to belong to the last stage of his life, when religion was occupying more and more of his thoughts. Eusebius gives an ecstatic account of the elderly Emperor delivering lengthy discourses on the faith to large audiences of officials, and, when they dutifully cheered, bidding them turn their eyes upwards and honour with their praises the King of all. Towards the end of his speeches he would speak of the divine judgement and inveigh against covetousness and extortion, to the embarrassment of many present: Eusebius regretfully records that though some amended their ways, the majority, after loudly clapping the Emperor's discourse, persisted in their evil courses.

It was by more material means, however, that Constantine chiefly promoted the diffusion of Christianity. He naturally preferred to employ Christians in his own service when he could, and though the majority of the officials were probably pagan, many Christians, often of quite humble origin, were promoted to high positions: Ablabius, for instance, rose from being a junior clerk in the office of the governor of Crete to praetorian prefect of the East. Apart from this, Constantine was extremely lavish in granting titular dignities, which carried the same privileges and immunities as did actual tenure of an office; and in addition to creating scores of senators, titular ex-praetorian prefects and ex-provincial governors, and *perfectissimi*, he invented a new dignity, that of patrician, and enrolled so many members in the new order of Companions that it had to be divided into three classes. He was equally lavish in grants of money and land, distributing freely the proceeds of confiscation, both from the temples and from private individuals. Christian converts from the higher ranks of society undoubtedly profited most from the Emperor's liberality, and even Eusebius is moved to comment adversely on the host of spurious converts who imposed on the Emperor's good-natured credulity.

Not only individuals, but the communities of the empire, soon discovered that the profession of Christianity was a sure passport to the Emperor's favour. Maiuma, the port of the zealously pagan city of Gaza, secured the status of an independent city and the name of Constantia by professing the Christian faith. Antaradus, the mainland suburb of the island city of Aradus, burnt down its temples and secured its independence from Aradus under the title of Constantina. An inscription records Constantine's favourable reply to a petition for the rank of city from Orcistus, a village of the Phrygian city of Nacoleia; what chiefly moves him in their favour, he expressly states, is that 'all the inhabitants are stated to be followers of the most sacred religion'.

The story of Constantine's dealings with the Jews is a good illustration of his policy. Though for theological reasons he held them in detestation and publicly vilified them in his letter to the Churches on the date of Easter, his actual treatment of them was not oppressive. He abolished, it is true, their ancient immunity from membership of city councils, but when Christians were compelled to serve, Jews could hardly expect exemption; and he maintained the immunity of two or three persons in each city, and later extended it to all synagogue officials, thus giving them equal status with the Christian clergy. He was not, however, prepared to tolerate proselytism, and he penalized Jewish owners who circumcised their pagan or Christian slaves. And when an opportunity presented itself for launching a mission to convert the Jews, he subsidized it lavishly.

The story of this mission is a curious one, but Epiphanius, who has recorded it, had it from the lips of the principal actor, a certain Joseph, whom he knew intimately in his old age. This Joseph was a very important person in the Jewish community, being one of the 'apostles' of the patriarch Ellel, the hereditary head of all the Jews of the Roman Empire. Ellel, according to Joseph, was secretly converted on his death-bed, and called in the bishop of Tiberias, where he resided, in the guise of a doctor, and received baptism from him: only Joseph discovered what was going on through a crack in the door. When Ellel died a few days later, Joseph opened his safe and discovered in it copies of the gospels translated into Hebrew. These he secreted to prevent scandal, but out of curiosity he read them, and was, despite himself, impressed.

Presently Joseph was dispatched by the young patriarch, Ellel's son, on an official mission to Cilicia to collect tithes and first-fruits and to inspect the synagogues. Joseph was a great disciplinarian and made many enemies among the local synagogue officers, who spied on him in the hopes of obtaining some handle against him. To their triumph they detected him reading his Hebrew gospels, and Joseph was publicly scourged in a synagogue, and an attempt was made to drown him in the river Cydnus. He now determined to become a Christian openly and receive baptism. This interesting event was reported to the Emperor, who invited him to the court; the date of this visit is probably

335, for in that year Constantine issued a constitution intimating 'to the Jews and their elders and patriarchs that if anyone should henceforth dare to attack with stones or any other form of malice, as we have learned is now happening, any person who had abandoned their deadly sect and turned to the worship of God, he would be forthwith delivered to the flames and burned with all his accomplices'.

The Emperor graciously asked Joseph what favour he desired to receive, and Joseph modestly requested only imperial authorization to build churches in the principal Jewish towns and villages, notably Tiberias, Sepphoris, Nazareth and Capernaum. Constantine, however, would not take no for an answer, and granted Joseph the title of Companion, with a pension from the treasury, as well as offering to pay for the building of the churches. Despite violent local opposition, Joseph was able with official backing to convert a derelict temple at Tiberias, the Hadrianeum, into a church, and to build a small church at Sepphoris. The mission, however, was not successful, and Joseph migrated to Scythopolis, where he ended his days as a wealthy and respected citizen.

In the military organization of the Empire Constantine made two important interconnected changes. He created a large field army, and to command it he established two supreme commanders, the Master of the Infantry and the Master of the Cavalry. The first measure was not a complete innovation: as far back as the middle of the third century a central imperial reserve had been created. But Diocletian had devoted most of his energy to strengthening the permanent garrisons of the frontiers, and his field army seems to have consisted normally of only a few crack regiments, which were for special campaigns reinforced by detachments temporarily withdrawn from the frontiers. Constantine established a large field army on a regular establishment, partly by extensive recruiting among the German tribes and partly by depleting the frontier troops, and stationed it in cities in the interior of the Empire to be immediately available to meet attack from any quarter. The troops of this field army, known as *comitatenses*, that is the court troops, enjoyed superior privileges to the frontier troops, the *ripenses* or *limitanei*. To command the latter Constantine completed the system of *duces* which Diocletian had begun, dividing the whole frontier into zones, each under a *dux*. The *comitatenses* were placed under the newly created Masters of the Infantry and the Cavalry. The chief effect of this was to sunder more sharply than before the military from the

civil administration, and in particular to deprive the praetorian prefects of all military functions. The praetorian
prefects remained responsible for raising recruits through
conscription and for supplying rations from the land tax
and armaments from the state factories, which they still
controlled: to use modern terms, they still fulfilled the
functions of quartermaster-general and master-general of
the Ordnance. But they ceased to be concerned with discipline or with command in the field: the masters served as
the Emperor's chiefs of staff and adjutants-general.

Zosimus violently denounces these changes as the direct
cause of the ruin of the Roman army. The régiments of
the field army, he declares, were corrupted by the luxurious life of the provinces, and proved through their indiscipline an intolerable burden on the cities where they
were billeted; meanwhile, the barbarians broke through
the depleted frontier garrisons and ravaged unchecked.
The division of authority between the prefects and the
masters was fatal to discipline: in the good old days the
praetorian prefects had been able to enforce their disciplinary measures by withholding supplies. These strictures
were unrealistic. It was a hopeless task to attempt to hold
the whole frontier in force: neither the man-power nor
the finances of the empire could support such a burden.
Moreover, experience had proved that static frontier garrisons were very liable to deteriorate in quality; and if the
frontier armies degenerated more rapidly owing to the
withdrawal of their best elements, it is unlikely that they
would in any case have effectively held the barbarian attacks. The field army, for all Zosimus may say, remained
a fine fighting force: it prolonged the struggle in the West
for another century and a half and saved the Empire in the
East.

The later development of the office of Masters of the
Infantry and the Cavalry hardly concerns Constantine. In

his conception these officers evidently were intended to serve under the immediate command of the Emperor – otherwise the division of authority by arms would have been unworkable. When later emperors ceased to take the field, the offices were combined, and this new office developed on very different lines in the western and eastern halves of the Empire. In the West there emerged one supreme commander, and he became the *de facto* ruler of the Empire, making and unmaking puppet emperors. In the East the command of the field army was divided territorially, with co-ordinate Masters for Illyricum, Thrace and the eastern frontier, besides two Masters commanding central reserves. This division of authority enabled the civil government to maintain control over the armies, and at the time proved satisfactory militarily.

In addition to this major reorganization Constantine made a minor military change, which was significant for the future. In 312 he disbanded the praetorian guard, which had been a crack corps picked from all the armies. For his bodyguard he created a new corps, known by the odd name of the Schools, recruited from Germans. This change is symptomatic of the increasing use of barbarian troops, and even whole barbarian tribes, in the imperial army. Constantine did not begin the practice, but he accelerated it, and perhaps went further than his predecessors in promoting Germans to high military commands and even to the greatest honours of the State: his nephew Julian reproaches him with having been the first to defile the consulate with a German. This policy did no harm so long as the German recruits were organized in Roman regiments under Roman officers, or even under German officers who had no special ties with them. The German danger began when after the battle of Adrianople in 378 whole tribes under their own chieftains were taken into Roman service as federates.

In the civil administration Constantine made few important or lasting changes. He felt the need for a closer control over the provincial administration, of whose corruption and oppressiveness he was only too well aware. This he endeavoured to achieve by substituting from time to time for the *vicarii* or deputy praetorian prefects who controlled each diocese his own Companions: thus we meet from time to time a Companion of Africa, of the Spains, of the Asiatic diocese and of the Orient, and the Emperor urges the provincials to make their complaints to these officers. This experiment was later abandoned, leaving one relic, that the Oriental diocese was controlled by an official with the title of Companion instead of *vicarius*.

In the central government Constantine created a new office, that of the Quaestor of the Sacred Palace. He was a kind of minister of justice, and his chief duty was to draft imperial constitutions. In the praetorian prefecture, apart from depriving the prefects of their military functions and making them purely civilian ministers, he made one experimental change, appointing a special praetorian prefect for the diocese of Africa. The other prefects seem, as hitherto, to have been attached to himself, as Augustus, and to his sons and his nephew Delmatius, who as Caesars administered parts of the Empire.

Constantine succeeded, where Diocletian had failed, in creating a stable and abundant gold currency. He started as early as 309 issuing a gold coin, the *solidus*, at 72 to the pound, but his success was mainly due to his confiscation of the temple treasures, which enabled him and his sons to keep up an abundant and pure issue. He also issued silver coins, apparently called *milliarenses*, in abundance. The silver currency proved difficult to manage owing to changes in the relative value of gold and silver, and was virtually abandoned after 395. The *solidus*, on the other hand, became the standard coin of the Byzantine Empire, and indeed of the Mediterranean world, for many centuries. The result of Constantine's creation of an abundant gold currency was that two generations later the imperial government was able to commute levies and payments in kind into gold, thus returning to a money economy, and that Roman coins regained their old reputation abroad. 'The second sign of sovereignty which God has granted to the Romans', wrote Cosmas two centuries later, 'is that all nations trade in their currency and in every place from one end of the world to the other [and Cosmas could speak with authority, having often sailed to India], it is acceptable and envied by every man and every kingdom, which thing does not apply to any other kingdom.'

Historians sometimes forget that by the early fifth century the Roman Empire once again enjoyed a money economy, and that the barbarian kingdoms which established themselves in the western parts inherited it. It was only in the dark ages which followed that western Europe gradually relapsed into the primitive system of payment in kind or by personal service which is called feudalism. In the East a stable currency encouraged an active commerce, which made Constantinople the richest city in the world, and an advanced fiscal system provided the Byzantine Empire with ample financial resources to resist Islam.

Constantine was excessively lavish in his expenditure. He poured out money on the erection of magnificent churches, on innumerable presents to individuals, on the maintenance of a sumptuous court, and above all on the building and adornment of his new capital on which he is said to have spent 60,000 pounds (by weight) of gold. He was equally lavish with his corn revenue, granting allocations to the churches and pensions to individuals, and instituting a free distribution of bread to 80,000 citizens of Constantinople. He also granted away crown lands freely to individual suitors and to endow the churches. It is little wonder that he was dubbed 'the prodigal'. By this extravagance Constantine rapidly exhausted the large reserves which Licinius, an exacting and parsimonious financier, had built up. When these were spent he fell back on sweeping confiscations: he extracted large quantities of gold from the temples, he probably seized the temple estates, and it may have been he who seized for the imperial treasury the local taxes which had been levied by the cities of the empire.

Despite these measures Constantine found the existing revenues inadequate for his cash expenditure, and he instituted two new taxes payable in money. The first, the *follis*, was a cash super-tax, graded according to the payer's landed property, on senators; as senators comprised the wealthiest men of the Empire, and as the ordinary land tax in kind was calculated on a flat rate, this was an eminently reasonable measure. The second, the *collatio lustralis*, was levied on all persons engaged in any form of trade, with the exception of farmers who sold their own produce. As the urban population of the Empire paid neither land tax nor poll tax, this measure also seems equitable enough. But it was extremely difficult to assess equitably, and, to make matters worse, it was collected at intervals of five years. Since the class of persons liable to the tax were mostly very poor, and had no reserve to draw upon, it proved extremely oppressive, and all the authorities, Christian and pagan alike, agree in painting a lurid picture of the terrible distress which was caused when the dreaded year came round.

Like all the later Roman emperors, Constantine waged a losing campaign against the greatest curse of the declining Empire – the corruption of the civil service. There was nothing which money could not obtain, and without money nothing could be obtained. Suitors could not gain admission in the law courts without feeing the numerous officials, and wealthy litigants could get their cases transferred to a distant, higher court beyond the means of their opponents. In the assessment of taxes and the allocation of *corvées*, the wealthy could always bribe the officials to transfer the burden to their humbler neighbours. Titular dignities carrying immunity from *corvées* and burdensome posts, such as membership of a town council, were freely bought and sold.

At times Constantine became quite hysterical in his impotent fury. 'Let the rapacious hands of the officials forthwith refrain,' he wrote in 331. 'Let them refrain, I repeat: for unless after this warning they do refrain, they will be cut off by the sword.' The Emperor goes on to demand in picturesque rhetoric that access to the court and the very sight of the judge shall not be put up to auction, and castigates individually the several officials, from those who introduced the litigants to those who supplied them with a record of judgement. If they demand money henceforth, he warns them that 'armed vengeance will visit them, which will sever the heads and necks of the villains', and if governors connive at their offences, they will be involved in a like fate. Constantine's bark was, however, worse than his bite: indeed, Eusebius' only criticism of his hero is that owing to his tender-hearted reluctance to inflict the death penalty, discipline was so relaxed as to reflect serious discredit on the whole administration. The same susceptibility to personal influence is to be seen in Constantine's lavish grants of immunity to his palatine officials, who with their sons and grandsons were excused *corvées* and requisitions, such as the provision of horses for the post, which burdened the ordinary citizen.

In Constantine's legislation it is difficult to trace much that is of distinctively Christian inspiration. In 325 he prohibited gladiatorial shows, and ordered that criminals formerly condemned to the arena should be sent to the mines; this law was enforced in the East, but in the West gladiatorial combats were not abolished till the beginning of the next century. Both in Africa and in Italy he ordered grants of money, food and clothing to be made from public funds to poor parents, who might otherwise be tempted to sell or expose their children: in this he was doubtless inspired by the example of the Church, though there was precedent for such measures in the pagan Empire of the second century. In several laws he displays an interest in the sanctity of marriage and a disapproval of irregular sex relations which is certainly due to Christian teaching. He tightened up the rules on divorce; women were no longer allowed to repudiate their husbands for drunkenness, gambling or running after other women, but only for murder, poisoning or tomb robbery, and men might divorce only for adultery, poisoning or procuring. Bastards were severely penalized, being denied all rights of inheritance from their fathers. Christian, too, is Constantine's anxiety to protect the modesty of women. In one law he insists that husbands shall in all legal proceedings represent their wives, 'lest women, on the pretext of conducting their cases, should irreverently rush into contempt for their modesty as matrons'. In another, officials collecting arrears are forbidden, under the threat of 'exquisite penalties', to drag married women out of their houses instead of distraining on their property. A more pleasing instance of interest in family life is a law prohibiting slave families to be broken up when the imperial estates to which they were attached were divided among several lessees.

Apart from this law, Constantine shows little sympathy for slaves. In a law dated 319 he ruled that if a slave died following a flogging or confinement in chains, his master was not liable to any charge: he was guilty of homicide only if he deliberately killed him or tortured him to death.

Unions between women and their slaves were brutally penalized, the woman being executed and the slave burned alive. Even when they had been manumitted, Constantine deprived them of their security by making them liable to re-enslavement if their former masters established that they were ungrateful or insolent. Nor did he show any sympathy to the vast mass of once free citizens who had been reduced to a kind of serfdom by being tied to their holdings. Of agricultural workers who had transferred their services to another landlord he writes in 332 : 'It will be appropriate that those who are planning escape should be put in chains like slaves, that they may be forced in virtue of a servile condemnation to fulfil those duties which are fitted for free men.'

Constantine's most celebrated achievement in the secular sphere, the foundation of Constantinople, receives curiously little notice in contemporary writers, and from the tangle of later legend it is difficult to unravel the precise significance of his action and his motives for it. Before attempting to do so one must appreciate the position which Rome held in the Empire. Rome was still the formal and sentimental capital. It was in no province, being subject to the jurisdiction of the Prefect of the City. It was the seat of the senate, and of the ancient republican magistrates, the consuls, the praetors and the quaestors. Its population, though all free inhabitants of the Empire were Romans, was regarded as being in a special sense the Roman people, and 120,000 of them enjoyed at the public expense free rations of bread and of pork in season.

Rome, however, had long ceased to be the administrative capital of the Empire. The administration followed the emperor, and the emperors had long lived a migratory life, visiting Rome only for brief periods. They had naturally often chosen favourite residences, where they lived when not on campaign or on tour through the provinces, and had built themselves palaces in these cities. Constantine, as Augustus of the Gauls, had usually lived in Trèves, and when after the conquest of the West he moved to Illyricum, Serdica became his favourite city – 'Serdica is my Rome' he is reported to have said. In the East, Diocletian had built himself a palace at Nicomedia, and his successors, Galerius and Licinius, had also usually resided there. There was nothing new, therefore, in an emperor's establishing a semi-permanent residence in some provincial city, and Nicomedia, close to Constantine's future capital, was already the normal seat of the senior Augustus. Still less was there any novelty in an emperor's giving his name to a city: the provinces were littered with cities bearing the name of almost every emperor from Augustus to Diocletian and Maximian.

It is not certain that Constantine officially styled his foundation 'the New Rome', but he granted it certain privileges which raised it above the ordinary ruck of provincial cities, though below Rome. Constantinople was endowed with a senate, but of a lower grade, whose members were entitled *clari* (distinguished) in contrast to genuine senators of Rome, who were *clarissimi* (most distinguished). Its population received 80,000 free rations of bread, the wheat for which was shipped from Egypt. The new foundation thus acquired a somewhat hybrid status. It did not supplant Rome as the formal capital of the Empire, or even attempt to rival it. But, on the other hand, it was more than the city which the emperor happened to make his favourite residence, possessing legal privileges which placed it outside the ordinary provincial administration.

Constantine seems to have decided thus to honour Byzantium directly after his victory over Licinius. He spared no expense in building the new city, and ransacked the temples of the pagan gods both for building material and for works of art to decorate its public places. The work of building took some six years, and the formal inauguration of Constantinople was celebrated on 11 May 330 with chariot races, preceded by a solemn procession. The birthday of the city was henceforth celebrated annually on this day, and in later times a gilded statue of the founder, holding in his right hand a gilded statuette of the Fortune of the City, was escorted in a chariot round the hippodrome by a column of troops in full ceremonial dress and holding candles, and as the statue passed the imperial box the reigning emperor saluted.

Constantine has left no record of his motives in founding his new capital save that in one of his constitutions he declares that he acted 'on the command of God'. This phrase should not be discounted as mere pious verbiage; for Constantine certainly believed that he received direct guidance from God in dreams. Constantinople must be regarded as a memorial and thank-offering for the final victory granted to Constantine by the Highest Divinity. By being dedicated to Him the new city was never sullied by pagan rites. This aspect of the new foundation, which is stressed by Eusebius, has been doubted, but on inadequate grounds. It is true that one or two pagan temples of Byzantium were allowed to survive, but there is no evidence that they were used for pagan cult. Constantine also built a temple to the Fortune of his new city, but this deity was a harmless abstraction, and once again there is no evidence that any cult was offered to her; this temple of the Fortune of Constantinople is analogous to the temples of the imperial cult which Constantine authorized elsewhere provided that no pagan ritual was practised in them. Nor again are the very secular rites whereby the city was inaugurated of significance; they were the common form for the inauguration of a new city, and, it must be remembered, no Christian ritual for such acts of state had as yet been evolved. Still less significant are the pagan rites which were privately practised in later days at the foot of the great porphyry column, on which stood a statue of Constantine wearing the radiate crown of Sol Invictus, and in the words of the inscription below, 'shining like the sun'. The inhabitants of Constantinople were, of course, by no means all Christians, and they could not be prevented from paying their devotions to the founder in their own fashion.

On the other hand, there is direct evidence that Constantine hoped to make Constantinople a Christian city, not only in the many churches that he built, but in a letter which he wrote to Eusebius, asking him to have prepared fifty copies of the scriptures on vellum, easy to read and convenient to handle, and to dispatch them forthwith in two public wagons to the capital. His reason, he states, is that 'in the city which bears our name, with the aid of the providence of the Saviour God, a very great number of people have dedicated themselves to the holy Church, so that as everything is going forward fast, it seems to me very proper that a greater number of churches should be built in it'.

Personal vanity doubtless played a large part in Constantine's giving a privileged status to the city which he had chosen for his residence and in squandering on its adornment the resources of the Empire. But Constantinople was not intended merely as a monument to its founder. The new city, never sullied with pagan rites, was designed to symbolize a break with the pagan past and the beginning of a new Christian empire.

Though Constantine chose the site to commemorate his victory over Licinius, its practical advantages must have influenced his decision. Strategically the new city was admirably placed within convenient distance of two of the major fronts of the Empire – the Danube and the eastern frontier against Persia. The Alps and the Rhine were, on the other hand, too distant for effective control, and the emperors who ruled at Constantinople had usually to delegate the defence of Italy and Gaul to a Caesar or another Augustus. Not only was the city a focus for the roads which linked Asia Minor and the East with Illyricum and the West, but by sea it was readily accessible from the central and eastern Mediterranean, and especially the great supply-provinces of Egypt. Tactically also Constantinople occupied a very strong position, lying on a promontory and thus liable to land attack only on one side, while against attack by sea it possessed outer defences in the narrow straits of the Bosphorus and the Hellespont, and in the Golden Horn a capacious harbour with an easily blocked entry.

The foundation of Constantinople probably hastened the collapse of the Roman Empire in the West. For the emperors who resided there controlled both the wealthy provinces of Asia Minor and the East, which contributed the greater part of the imperial revenues, and the Illyrian provinces, which long remained the Empire's best recruiting ground; and the emperors of the West were left with inadequate resources in money and manpower to withstand the pressure of the barbarians on the upper Danube and the Rhine. But the New Rome prolonged the life of the Empire in the East. To protect their capital the emperors were compelled, when the Balkans had been overrun, to hold eastern Thrace at all costs. They thus sealed against invasion the provinces of Asia Minor, which remained, even after Syria and Egypt had fallen to the Arabs, a rich reserve of men and money, and at the same time retained a bridgehead in Europe from which they reconquered the Balkans time and time again.

Constantinople became, as no other capital city has been, the heart of the Byzantine Empire. When all else was lost, hope still lived so long as the great city remained impregnable. In 616 the Avars had overrun the Balkan provinces and the Persians had swept over Syria, Egypt and Asia Minor. But for ten years Constantinople held out, and it was from its harbours that Heraclius embarked on the campaigns which finally humbled Persia. In 668-75 the city resisted for seven years the huge naval armament launched against it by the Caliphate, then at the height of its power, and fifty years later it withstood a yet more formidable attack by the Arabs, both by land and by sea. Constantinople was not to fall to a foreign invader till in 1203 the Venetians treacherously diverted the Fourth Crusade against the bulwark of Christendom. Even after this disaster it was to resist the Turks for two and a half centuries before, with all the Balkans and Anatolia already subdued, it at last fell in 1453 to Mahomet the Conqueror. Even under Muslim dominion it remained the spiritual capital, not only of the ancient Eastern Churches, but of the great Slav Churches far beyond the bounds of the Empire which it had founded.

15 Constantine's Baptism

Shortly after Easter 337 Constantine fell ill. He moved from the capital to a neighbouring thermal spa to take the waters, and thence to his mother's city of Helenopolis, where he prayed in the great church that she had built in honour of Lucian of Antioch and the other martyrs who had suffered there. Then, realizing that his last hour was near, he travelled towards Nicomedia, and in a suburb of that city he called together a number of bishops. He had hoped, he said, to receive the seal of immortality in the River Jordan, where our Saviour had been baptized, but God had thought otherwise: let there be no hesitation, for even if the Lord of life and death should grant him a further span of life he was determined to live henceforth as a member of the Church and to share its prayers. The Emperor laid aside his purple, and donning the white robe of a catechumen received baptism at the hands of Eusebius, the bishop of Nicomedia. A few days later, at midday on Whitsunday, he died.

He had previously made arrangements for the succession. His three surviving sons, Constantine, Constantius and Constans, and his nephew Delmatius were already as Caesars administering the parts of the Empire to which they were to succeed. Pending the arrival of his sons, Constantine's body was conveyed to Constantinople, and there lay in state, clad once more in the imperial purple, on a golden bier in the great hall of the palace, to be adored by the generals, Companions and civil officials whose privilege it had been to attend his levees while he lived, by the members of the senate and other dignitaries, and finally by the common people with their wives and children. At length Constantius, the second son, arrived from Antioch, and Constantine's body was laid in the sarcophagus which he had prepared for himself between the twelve cenotaphs of the Apostles in the great basilica which he had dedicated in their honour.

It may seem strange that 'the servant of God', who claimed to have been 'appointed by God to be bishop of those without' the Church, and had summoned and presided as one of themselves over a universal synod of bishops, did not become a full member of the Church till the hour of his death. But in this Constantine was not exceptional. In his day, and indeed down to the end of the fourth century, many pious Christians remained catechumens all their lives. Baptism was not regarded, it would seem, as the ceremony of admission to the church – catechumens were ordinarily spoken of as Christians – but as a solemn rite which cleansed the Christian of sin and made him one of 'the faithful', an inner group of initiates sometimes distinguished from ordinary Christians. Constantine certainly regarded himself as a Christian, and no ordinary one. God had vouchsafed to him a celestial vision, had revealed to him the Sign whereby he had triumphed over all his enemies, and had entrusted to him the sovereignty of the whole Empire. We know from his own words that he felt personally responsible to God for maintaining the peace of the Church and for weaning his pagan subjects from their errors. In his public capacity he regarded himself as holding a commission from God co-ordinate with if not superior to that of the bishops. And 't must be remembered that the bishops accepted this position. They not only accepted but solicited his judgements on ecclesiastical affairs. None is recorded to have been tactless enough to rebuke or even to correct the imperial convert, but many were eager to load him with panegyrics – at his Tricennalia one of the bishops congratulated Constantine that in his present life he had been thought worthy of universal imperial sovereignty and in the life to come he would reign side by side with the Son of God.

But if Constantine felt himself in his public capacity to hold a special relationship to God, he may well, as his acquaintance with Christian doctrine became fuller, have had doubts about his personal salvation. We unfortunately know practically nothing about Constantine's personal religion. In his theological learning rapid progress can be traced from the moment when he came to the East. He was then, as his letter to Alexander and Arius shows, blissfully ignorant of theology. Three months after the Council of Nicaea in his letter to the Nicomedians, he is not afraid to set forth the orthodox doctrine, and in his letter to Arius in 333 he confidently crosses swords with the heresiarch. He may, of course, have got his theological arguments prepared for him by experts, but Eusebius testifies that he used to sit up late into the night studying the scriptures and listen zealously to sermons. He tells of a sermon which he himself preached in the palace : Constantine insisted, greatly to Eusebius' embarrassment, in standing like the rest of the congregation, and as the sermon was very long Eusebius endeavoured to cut it short, but the Emperor insisted on hearing it through, and remained standing to the end. Constantine also studied contemporary theological works. We possess a letter from Constantine to Eusebius thanking him for a treatise on the meaning of the Easter festival, and asking for similar works from his pen. It is of interest that Constantine had this treatise translated into Latin, which he read more easily than Greek : he expresses satisfaction that Eusebius approves the official translator's accuracy, while apologizing for his incapacity to reproduce the literary elegance of the original. Constantine himself wrote a theological treatise in Latin, entitled *Of the Gathering of the Saints*, which was officially translated into Greek. A Greek treatise under that title is preserved in some manuscripts of Eusebius, but its authenticity is very dubious.

Constantine seems, to judge by his language, to have conceived of God mainly as a God of power. His favourite expressions are the Mighty One, the Greatest or the Highest God, the Lord of all, God Almighty, God the all-seeing, and he represents Him as giving victory to His servants and casting down His enemies to destruction. Only rarely does he speak of Him as the Saviour, and never as loving or compassionate. Twice only does he refer to God as the Father, and on both occasions he seems to envisage Him as the stern possessor of *patria potestas* rather than as a loving protector of his children – 'So will you win the grace and favour of the Lord and Father of all,' he writes and 'God the Founder and Father of all, whom many of the previous Roman emperors, led astray by frantic error, strove to deny, but an avenging fate consumed them all'.

Christianity was to Constantine pre-eminently a true belief and a divine law. The content of this law he defines thus in his letter to Sapor:

He demands from men only a pure heart and an unspotted soul, weighing acts of virtue and piety in these terms. He is pleased with deeds of kindness and gentleness, approving the mild and hating the violent, loving faith and punishing faithlessness: shattering all boastful power, He takes vengeance on the insolence of the proud, and utterly destroys those who are lifted up by vanity, but gives a fitting reward to the humble and long-suffering.

In other passages Constantine depicts God as dispensing rewards and punishments not only in this world but the next. 'The Highest God is the lord of judgement,' he writes, and he alludes frequently to the glorious honours which the faithful, and especially the confessors and martyrs, are to receive hereafter, and to 'the places of punishment beneath the earth' and 'eternal punishment in the depths of Acheron'.

Knowing his own violent and imperious temper, Constantine may well have doubted his capacity to keep 'the divine law'. In particular a domestic tragedy which occurred the year after the Council of Nicaea may have gravely shaken him. We know very little of it, for contemporary authors studiously ignore it – Eusebius, in the last edition of his *Church History*, carefully deleted the passages where he had even mentioned one of the victims – and we have only untrustworthy gossip from later historians. All we know for certain is that the Caesar Crispus, Constantine's brilliant eldest son, who had recently distinguished himself in the campaign against Licinius, was without warning, as he was accompanying his father to the Vicennalia celebrations at Rome, executed at Pola; and that shortly afterwards the empress Fausta, recently proclaimed Augusta, was mysteriously put to death – rumour said by suffocation in the hot chamber of her bath. The story in the later authors is that Fausta, jealous of the popularity of her stepson, accused him of having attempted to seduce her, and that the Emperor's mother, Helena, to avenge her favourite grandson, either convinced Constantine that Fausta was the guilty party in the alleged affair, or, according to another version, accused her of adultery with a palace official.

That Fausta was charged with adultery is suggested by a constitution, posted at Nicomedia on 25 April 326. In this Constantine limits the right of accusation in case of adultery to the near relatives of the erring wife, and in the first place to her husband – in Roman law adultery was a crime, and a common informer had hitherto been able to accuse. It may be, too, that Helena played some part in her fall. It is, at any rate, odd that Helena was proclaimed Augusta – thus emerging from an eclipse of over thirty years – only a year or two before Fausta's death, and it is perhaps significant that immediately after she made a pilgrimage to Palestine – she had been converted to Christianity by her son, Eusebius tells us – where she contributed lavishly to the new churches at the holy places. She died not long after in the odour of sanctity.

A clue to Crispus' offence is perhaps to be found in an extraordinary edict which Constantine issued from Aquileia on 1 April 326. In it he imposes 'most savage penalties' (they are not on record, having been reduced later to capital punishment) on abduction, and this whether the girl was willing or unwilling; in the former case she is to suffer the same penalty as her paramour, in the latter she is still to be penalized by the loss of her rights of inheritance, because she could have roused the neighbours by her cries. The girl's parents, if they condone the offence, are to be deported. Servants who acted as go-betweens are to have their mouths closed with molten lead. The date and the place at which this edict was issued, and its violent, almost hysterical, tone, strongly suggest that it was provoked by Crispus' case. But if this is so, Crispus' offence cannot have been that alleged by later popular report. It would rather seem that he had abducted some unknown girl, and that she had acquiesced and the parents had been willing to compromise the case. Crispus' offence was the graver, in that he was already married to a certain Helena, and had a child by her – born in 322. He can thus have offered satisfaction to the unknown girl only by making her his concubine; and that this is what he had done is suggested by another law, issued about this time and perhaps forming part of the edict on abduction, prohibiting married men from keeping concubines.

On the whole, then, it would seem unlikely that the melodramatic story recounted by later writers is true; the cases of Crispus and Fausta were unconnected, despite their coincidence in time. The two tragedies must have been a grave shock to public feeling, and it is easy to understand how popular rumour would inevitably have linked them. Later pagan legend, hostile to Constantine's memory, went further still. It represents Constantine as harrowed by remorse when he found that he had precipitately killed his innocent son on a false charge, and seeking everywhere some rite whereby he could expiate his sin. The pagan hierophants sternly declared that they knew of no purification for so heinous an offence, but a Christian priest told Constantine that baptism would wash away any sin. And so it was, declared the pagan writers of the next century, that Constantine became a Christian.

What Constantine's real feelings were we do not know. He never rehabilitated the memory of either Crispus or Fausta: their names were erased from public inscriptions and never restored, their effigies disappeared from the coins and were never recalled by any commemorative issues – till after Constantine's death Fausta's sons placed their mother's image on their coinage. But although he never publicly admitted that he was wrong, Constantine may well have felt some sense of remorse and even of guilt. For whatever the truth of the charges, he had in a moment of passion, without pausing for reflection or allowing time for repentance, killed his son and his wife.

Constantine's exceptional tenderness to the Novatians, whom he released from the penalties falling on other heretics a few months after the deaths of Crispus and Fausta, suggests that he may have had a lurking fear that their stern view was right, that there was no forgiveness for mortal sin except through baptism. Such a view accorded with Constantine's own conception of God as the all-powerful and all-seeing judge, Who visited all those who offended against His laws with utter destruction upon earth, and with 'eternal punishment in the depths of Acheron'. Baptism, 'the seal which gives immortality', blotted out all sins, however heinous; was it not safer to postpone baptism till one could sin no more.

16 Constantine's Place in History

Constantine hardly deserves the title of 'Great' which posterity has given him, either by his character or by his abilities. He lacked firmness of purpose to pursue steadily his long-term objectives. His temper was tempestuous, and in his violent outbursts of rage he would make hasty decisions and utter savage threats, which he fortunately did not usually fulfil. He was highly susceptible to flattery, and fell completely under the influence of any dominating personality who happened to be at his side. He shows up best as a general: in war his rapidity and boldness of decision carried the day, and his campaigns against Maxentius and Licinius were brilliant. His general strategical conceptions for the defence of the empire were also sound. In the more humdrum task of administration he was weak: he sincerely wished – like all the later emperors – to cleanse the Augean stable of the civil service, to make justice accessible to all and to distribute fairly the burden of taxation between rich and poor; but he had not the strength of mind to enforce his own rules, oscillating between threats of fantastic penalties and weak condonation of offences. In this sphere his susceptibility to personal influence was ruinous: he lavished privileges on his palatine officials and was reluctant to punish the worst offenders among them. In finance he was ruinously extravagant: perhaps the greatest need of the Empire was to cut down its overhead costs, but he spent with a reckless prodigality which made the already scarcely tolerable burden of the peasantry beyond their endurance. His ecclesiastical policy exhibits the same defects. He had a noble objective, the unity of the Church, but in pursuing it he oscillated helplessly between the various parties, now condemning one and now another in alternate fits of rage.

Still less does Constantine deserve the title of 'Saint', which the Eastern Church has bestowed upon him. He was, it is true, according to his lights, a good man on the whole, though his political murders – particularly that of Licinius – shocked even contemporary opinion, and his execution of his wife and son was felt by many to be an inexpiable stain on his character. His sexual life seems to have been impeccable. Even in his pagan days his panegyrists go out of their way to praise his continence: he married young, according to one, to avoid even the venial errors of youth and thus presented the strange spectacle of an uxorious young man. By contrast with many of his contemporaries, who used their imperial power to gratify their lusts, he was a prodigy. He was also, it would appear, in general a kind-hearted man, too kind-hearted to enforce proper discipline, and his intentions towards all his subjects were good. But he was no saint: his relations with his God were regulated by fear and hope and not by love.

To the other title which the Orthodox Church has bestowed upon him, 'the Peer of the Apostles', he has a better claim, for his career profoundly influenced the history of the Church and the future of Christianity.

Some conflict and some adjustment there was bound to be between Church and State if any emperor turned Christian. In the Greek and Roman conception of the State, religion was a department, and a very important one, of government. It was one of the prime duties of the government to maintain the peace of the gods, and the Roman senate in particular had always attached great importance to the expiation of prodigies and unfavourable omens, to the ascertainment of the will of the gods by auspices, and in general to the meticulous performance by the magistrates, assisted by experts such as soothsayers and priests, of the traditional rites. The Roman emperors had inherited this tradition, and the history of the persecutions shows that in the third century they took their duties seriously. Moreover, the emperors considered it their duty, after due consultation with experts, to decide what was pleasing to the gods. There had never been a priestly caste in Rome: the pontifices and the augurs and the rest were lay experts on religion just as the jurisconsults were lay experts on law, men whose opinion was valued by the government but not accepted as infallible.

The Church, on the other hand, had grown up as a furtive society of questionable legality, subject from time to time to repressive action by the authorities. In these circumstances it had developed its own organization and its own methods of deciding what doctrine and worship were pleasing to God. It had its infallible scriptures, its tradition and its system of episcopal councils for resolving differences of opinion and practice. When the emperor became a Christian, there was bound sooner or later to be a conflict between his claim to decide what measures should be taken to ensure God's favour for the Empire and the claim of the Church to decide what Christians must believe and do. Much would depend on the character of the first Christian emperor.

The leaders of the Church were slow to realize the danger. In the days before the Great Persecution, they had not scrupled to invoke a pagan emperor: when Paul, bishop of Antioch, had refused when condemned by a synod to vacate his church, his opponents had appealed to Aurelian and had accepted his ruling that the bishop approved by those of Italy and Rome should have possession. Constantine was the champion and benefactor of the Church, and it is perhaps not surprising that the bishops submitted their disputes to him. The Donatists invoked his judgement again and again – it was only when the imperial government had irrevocably decided against them that they developed a doctrine of ecclesiastical independence and denounced their Catholic opponents for calling in the secular arm. The Melitians frequently appealed to Constantine against Athanasius, and the Eusebian party induced him to convoke the Councils of Caesarea and Tyre while Athanasius himself appealed to him against the Council of Tyre. Only at the Council of Antioch did the Eusebian bishops endeavour to check appeals to the Emperor against councils; Athanasius did not develop scruples against the secular power till after Constantine's death the imperial government was fully committed to the opposite cause.

For his part Constantine had no doubts about his imperial duty. It was his task to secure God's favour on the empire by securing, by force if necessary, that His subjects worshipped God in a manner pleasing to Him. This was the traditional duty of a Roman emperor, but Constantine, from the peculiar circumstances of his conversion, undertook it without hesitation. He was no contrite sinner, convinced that the Church opened the way of salvation. He had been vouchsafed a heavenly vision by God Himself, who had entrusted to him, His servant, the governance of all earthly things. As the Emperor appointed by God, it was his right and duty to impose God's will upon His Church.

He deferred in general to the opinion of experts – indeed, he expresses an implicit faith in the divine inspiration of assemblies of bishops – but he arrogated the right of convening these assemblies and dictating their composition, of guiding their deliberations and of reviewing their decisions. And by being the first to convene a general council of the whole Church, he established a precedent, unquestioned for centuries and still maintained by the Eastern Church, that only the emperor can call a general council. He deposed and exiled bishops, not only when condemned by a council, but on his own authority, and he went very near to appointing bishops, as when he disapproved of the choice made by the Council of Antioch and suggested two other candidates from whom they might choose. Finally he issued penal laws against dissenting sects without formal authorization by any council, depriving the Donatists and the various Eastern heretical groups of their buildings and banning their religious gatherings; and relieved of their penalties the Novatians whom he personally respected.

Not only did the Church acquiesce in these actions, but, if Eusebius be accepted as its spokesman, it approved the doctrine from which they proceeded. In the panegyric which he composed for the Emperor's Tricennalia, Eusebius likens Constantine to 'a praetorian prefect of the Great King,' destroying the images of the demons whom Christ has vanquished, and to 'a spokesman of the Universal King,' who 'calls all his flock to the knowledge of the truth'. It is the Word of God, he declares, 'from Whom and through Whom, in the likeness of the kingdom on high, the Emperor, the friend of God, holds the tiller of all earthly things and steers them in imitation of the Mighty One,' and he proceeds to draw an elaborate and to our ears slightly blasphemous analogy between the functions of the Word and of 'the Emperor His friend' in fulfilling God's will in heaven and on earth respectively.

Thus was born Caesaropapism, the doctrine that the secular sovereign is by the grace of God supreme governor of the Church within his dominions and is as such divinely authorized to dictate the religious beliefs of his subjects.

In the Byzantine Empire and in its spiritual heir, Russia, this doctrine was implicitly accepted. In western Europe it was during the Middle Ages vigorously and in the main successfully challenged by the Papacy, which arrogated to itself the imperial function. With the Reformation it raised its head once more, not only in the Protestant states, where, under the name of Erastianism, it became accepted doctrine, but also to a lesser extent in Catholic lands, whose kings treated their national Churches more and more as departments of state.

For the whole future of Christianity Constantine's conversion was even more momentous. It may be argued indeed that the Roman Empire must eventually have become Christian, and that an emperor must at last have been converted. But there are no solid grounds for this belief. In the contemporary Empire of Persia, Christian churches were numerous, and despite, or because of, periodical persecutions, increased and flourished; but no Persian king was converted, and the Christians remained a small minority in the Persian dominions. Later, when the Christian lands of Syria, Egypt and North Africa fell under Muslim rule, within three or four centuries Christians had merely by social pressure – for persecution was rare – become an insignificant minority once more.

It may be argued that Zoroastrianism and Islam were tougher antagonists than the amorphous paganism of the Roman Empire. But paganism showed a surprising vitality – it had, like modern Hinduism, the great asset of catering for every taste, and it was deeply interwoven with the glorious traditions of the classical world. And whatever its attraction it did survive for centuries, despite the social pressure exercised by a Christian government and penal laws. In 542, over two centuries after the whole Empire had come under Christian rule, Justinian found it necessary to appoint John, bishop of Ephesus, as missionary to the pagans in Asia, Lydia, Caria and Phrygia, and in this small area of western Asia Minor, one of the oldest centres of Christianity, he found over 70,000 pagans to baptize, mainly it would seem in the remote rural areas. Four years later John was given a similar mission in Constantinople itself, the Christian city *par excellence*, and found many crypto-pagans in the professional classes – professors of literature and rhetoric, lawyers and doctors – and in the official aristocracy, including the Prefect of the City himself. Thirty years later another inquisition revealed a multitude of pagans in Syria and Mesopotamia, including the governor of this last province. In these areas paganism survived into Arab times; the pagans of Mesopotamia retained for themselves the privileges of 'a people of the book' by dubbing themselves Sabians, and the Shia sects of Syria have strong Neoplatonic elements in their doctrines.

But hypothetical history is not a very useful pursuit. The facts are that Constantine, converted by an accident in his youth, united the whole Empire under his rule and reigned gloriously for twenty-five years. He brought up his three sons to be pious Christians, and the last of them reigned for another twenty-five years, having ultimately reunited the Empire under his rule. During that half-century the Church had enjoyed imperial protection, paganism had been viewed with disfavour. Christians had been promoted and pagans frowned upon. By Constantius' death the work had been done too well for Julian, in his brief reign of eighteen months ending in defeat and disaster, to undo it: the army chiefs on his death elected a Christian emperor, and thereafter no pagan was to wear the purple.

Christianity thus became the official, and gradually also the normal, religion of the Roman Empire. The effect on the Church was mainly bad. As converts came in no longer by conviction, but for interested motives or merely by inertia, the spiritual and moral fervour of the Church inevitably waned. To the Empire the official change of religion made little difference: the old corruption and oppression of the masses by officials and landlords went on unabated, and the last remnants of public spirit faded away. Nor is this surprising for the object of the Church was not to reform the Empire but to save souls. To contemporary Christian thought the things of this world were of little moment, and the best Christian minds preferred not to touch the pitch of public life lest they be defiled. Men of high conviction and character became bishops or hermits, and government was left in the main to careerists.

Nevertheless, to the future of Christianity its official adoption by the Empire was momentous, for Christianity thus acquired the prestige and glamour of the Roman name; it became synonymous with that ancient civilization whose grandiose buildings, stately ceremonial, luxurious life and ordered discipline fascinated the uncouth barbarians of the north. The Germans had at first been mere brigands, but soon they hankered to enter the charmed circle of the Roman world, their kings to become marshals of the Empire and their warriors great landlords like the senatorial aristocracy. Inevitably they copied Roman ways, and with the rest of Roman culture adopted the Roman religion.

The tribes who first infiltrated into the Empire and established principalities in its western provinces, the Visigoths, the Vandals and the Ostrogoths, were already Christians before they entered imperial territory, though, like the later conquerors of Italy, the Lombards, they were unfortunately Arians, having been converted while the Empire was in the Arian phase which followed Constantine's death. The Vandals in Africa and the Ostrogoths in Italy were eliminated by the great restorer of the Roman

Empire, Justinian, before they could conform to the now dominant Catholic faith, but the Visigoths in Spain, and the Lombards who succeeded the Ostrogoths in Italy, succumbed to the pressure of the Roman name and became Catholics. The more barbarous Franks, who were still pagans when they overran Gaul, forthwith adopted the Catholic faith under the leadership of their king Clovis, and the even more uncouth Angles and Saxons who had occupied Britain were converted by the rival efforts of the Irish Church and the Roman mission of Pope Gregory the Great. The conversion of the Franks and of the English proved important, for it was English missionaries who first evangelized the heathen tribes of Germany, and the Frankish king Charles the Great who launched the great series of crusades which finally brought them within the Catholic Church. In the next century the heathen Slavs who had overrun the Balkans yielded to the missionary efforts of Constantine's New Rome, and at the end of the tenth century the splendours of Constantinople so impressed Vladimir, Prince of Kief, that he with all his people was baptized, and the conversion of Russia was begun.

Thus though Christianity lost its original homeland to Islam, its future was safe in the hands of the European nations, who were to carry it to the New World. If Constantine had not seen his heavenly vision of the Cross, would this have come about?

Note on Books

To readers who wish to delve deeper into Constantine's own story, my best advice is to study Professor N. H. Baynes's masterly monograph, 'Constantine the Great and the Christian Church' (*Proceedings of the British Academy*, XV 1929, also published separately by Humphrey Milford), and then to read for themselves the works of the Church Fathers mentioned in the Introduction, most of which are available in English translations. In the two existing English lives of Constantine by J. B. Firth (*Constantine the Great*, London, 1905) and G. P. Baker (*Constantine the Great and the Christian Revolution*, London, 1931) they will not find much that is not in this book, and of the two recent French lives by J. Maurice (*Constantin le grand et l'origine de la civilisation chrétienne*, Paris, 1925) and A. Piganiol (*L'empereur Constantin*, Paris, 1932) the former is uncritically pious and the latter perversely clever.

Those who wish to pursue the ecclesiastical history of the age should consult B. J. Kidd's *A History of the Church to A.D. 461* (Oxford, 1922), or in French, volumes II and III of *Histoire de l'église depuis les origines jusqu' à nous jours*, edited by A. Fliche and V. Martin; *De la fin du 2e siècle à la paix constantinienne* (Paris, 1935), by J. Lebreton and J. Zeiller, and *De la paix constantinienne à la mort de Théodose* (Paris, 1936), by P. de Labriolle, G. Bardy and J. R. Palanque. Volume II has been translated into English as *The History of the Primitive Church*, volumes III and IV. An old but good book on the Arian controversy is H.M. Gwatkin's *Studies of Arianism* (London, 1900); the latest study of the Council of Nicæa and its aftermath is A. E. Burn's *The Council of Nicæa* (London, 1925), an excellent little book.

For the general history of the age Gibbon's *Decline and Fall of the Roman Empire* (best read in J. B. Bury's edition – London, 1896 and later – which corrects the surprisingly few errors of fact,) is still the best introduction. The reader should, however, be forewarned against Gibbon's great weakness, which is not so much anti-Christian bias as a temperamental incapacity to understand religion: to Gibbon's eighteenth-century rationalism a religious man was either a fool or a knave. The most recent and authoritative history in English is the twelfth volume of the *Cambridge Ancient History: The Imperial Crisis and Recovery* (Cambridge, 1939), which covers the period from the accession of Septimius Severus (A.D. 193) to the eve of the Council of Nicæa (A.D. 324). The *Cambridge Ancient History* overlaps with the first volume of the *Cambridge Medieval History: The Christian Roman Empire and the Foundation of the Teutonic Kingdoms* (Cambridge, 1911). In the French *Histoire Générale*, edited by G. Glotz, the relevant volumes are IV, i, *L'empire romain de l'avènement des Sévères au concile de Nicée* (Paris, 1937), by M. Besnier, and IV, ii, *L'empire chrètien (325–395)* (Paris, 1947), by A. Piganiol. Covering shorter periods there are H. M. D. Parker's *A History of the Roman World A.D. 138–337* (London, 1935), and for a rather later period (A.D. 395–565) J. B. Bury's *History of the Later Roman Empire* (second edition, London, 1923), and, extending even later, down to Charlemagne, H. St. L. B. Moss's *The Birth of the Middle Ages* (Oxford, 1935), a most stimulating and readable book.

Some More Recent Books

Since the appearance of this book, Professor Jones has produced the most comprehensive treatment available in English of the social and administrative background to the age of Constantine: *The Later Roman Empire, 284–602: A Social, Economic and Administrative Survey*, 3 vols., Oxford, 1964, of which the substance is available in abbreviated form as *The Decline of the Ancient World*, London, 1966. His paper 'The Social Background of the Struggle between Paganism and Christianity' in *The Conflict between Christianity and Paganism*, ed. A. D. Momigliano, Oxford, 1963, develops some themes of the book. Papers in the same collection, by A. D. Momigliano, 'Pagan and Christian Historiography in the Fourth Century' and J. Vogt, 'Pagans and Christians in the Family of Constantine', are relevant. P. Brown, *The World of Late Antiquity*, London, 1971, pays more attention to the cultural and intellectual background, and provides a select bibliography on a wide range of subjects. An excellent conspectus of recent work is to be found in

Dumbarton Oaks Papers, vol. 21, Washington, 1967: John L. Teall, 'The Age of Constantine: Change and Continuity in Administration and Economy'; Johannes A. Straub, 'Constantine as ΚΟΙΝΟΣ ΕΠΙΣΚΟΠΟΣ: Tradition and Innovation in the Representation of the First Christian Emperor's Majesty', Evelyn B. Harrison, 'The Constantinian Portrait'; Irving Lavin, 'The Ceiling Paintings in Trier and Illusionism in Constantinian Painting'; R. Krautheimer, 'The Constantinian Basilica'. The last four of these papers show how much may yet be learnt about the personality and aims of Constantine from a closer study of cross-currents in Roman art and culture of the early fourth century A.D. than have, until now, been considered in most accounts of the reign of Constantine.

The Roman Imperial Coinage, ed. C. H. V. Sutherland and R. A. G. Carson, vol. 7, by P. M. Bruun, *Constantine and Licinius* (A.D. 303–337), London, 1967, is a fundamental account. R. MacMullen, *Constantine*, New York, 1970, is a colourful evocation. J. Vogt, *Reallexikon für Antike und Christentum*, vol. 3, Stuttgart, 1957, cols. 306–79 provides a reliable guide to the vast literature in all languages on Constantine – among which A. Piganiol, *L'Empire chrétiens* (Histoire Romaine IV, 2) Paris, 1947, remains, in many ways the most acute and informative. Basic sources for the history of the Church have recently been published, notably Eusebius, *The History of the Church*, Penguin Classics: London, 1965 and *The Roman State and the Christian Church, a Collection of Documents up to A.D. 535*, ed. T. R. Coleman–Norton, 3 vols., London, 1966. W. H. C. Frend, *Martyrdom and Persecution in the Early Church*, Oxford, 1965, and E. R. Dodds, *Pagans and Christians in an Age of Anxiety*, Cambridge, 1965, provide sharply contrasted views of the religious evolution of the third century: on these accounts and their implications for the conversion of Constantine, see especially P. Brown, 'Approaches to the Religious Crisis of the Third Century A.D.' *English Historical Review*, 83, 1968. D. S. Wallace–Hadrill, *Eusebius of Caesarea*, London, 1960, is a useful monograph.

P.B.

1971

Chronological Tables
and Constantine's
Family Tree

Secular affairs   a. = augustus, c. = caesar

The west   **The east**

---

284   *17 Sept 284: Accession of Diocletian a.*   284

286   *1 Mar 286: Maximian proclaimed*   286
                       caesar (later augustus)

    Maximian a.   Diocletian a.

293   *1 Mar 293: Proclamation of the*   293
                       caesars

    Maximian a.   Diocletian a.
    Constantius c.   Galerius c.

305   Constantius a., Severus c.   *1 May: abdication of the augusti*   305
       25 July 306: Constantine proclaimed 23 Oct: Maxentius proclaimed   305
       Constantine a.   Galerius a.
       (till 307 c.)   *11 Nov 308: congress of Carnuntum*   Maximin c.   308
       Maxentius a.   Galerius a.
       (Maximian a.   Licinius a.
       307–310)   *May 311: death of Galerius*   Maximin a.   311
312   *28 Oct 312:⤬ Milvian Bridge*   Licinius a.   312
313   *Feb 313: Conference of Milan   30 April:⤬ Hadrianople* Maximin a.   313
314   *8 Oct 314:⤬ Cibale*   314

    Constantine a.   Licinius a.

324   *18 Sept 324:⤬ Chrysopolis*   324

330   *11 May 330: Inauguration of Constantinople*   330

    Constantine a.   Constantine a.

337   *22 May 337: Death of Constantine*   337

Constantine's Family Tree

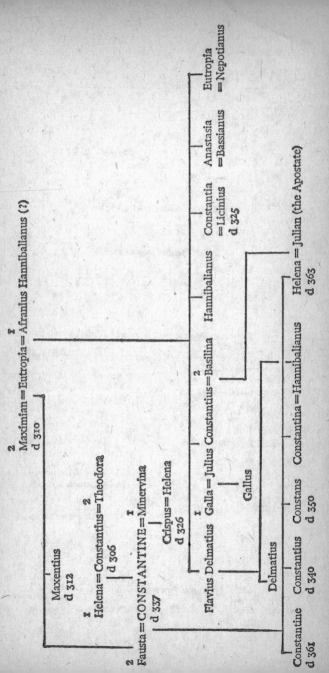

Index

Teach Yourself History
in Pelicans

THE USE OF HISTORY*   *A. L. Rowse*
'History is a delightful study, and Mr Rowse a delightful guide' – C. V. Wedgwood

JULIUS CAESAR AND ROME*   *J. P. V. D. Balsdon*
Julius Caesar is shown for what he was – cultured, generous, often unprincipled and, until the end, a lucky man.

WYCLIFFE AND ENGLISH NON-CONFORMITY*   *K. B. McFarlane*
The dramatic story of the great fourteenth-century Oxford scholar who initiated the first English revolt against the supreme authority of Rome.

MACHIAVELLI AND RENAISSANCE ITALY*
J. R. Hale
This biography illustrates the importance of the influence of Machiavelli's practical political experience on his contribution to political theory.

ELIZABETH I AND THE UNITY OF ENGLAND*
Joel Hurstfield
The personality of this great queen stands out against the background of her remarkable contemporaries.

THOMAS JEFFERSON AND AMERICAN DEMOCRACY*   *Max Beloff*
Thomas Jefferson contributed more than any other thinker or statesman to shaping the ideals and political techniques of modern America.

LENIN AND THE RUSSIAN REVOLUTION
Christopher Hill
A penetrating study of Lenin and the revolution that was his life's work.

*Not for sale in the U.S.A.